The Autł

Susan Singleton, LLB, is a solicitor with her own firm, Singletons, which specialises in competition law, both UK and EC, intellectual property (including computer law) and general commercial law. She writes for a wide range of legal periodicals and is a frequent speaker both in the UK and abroad.

Susan is a member of the the Solicitors' European Group, the Institute of Export and is contributing author to many Croner reference books, including *Croner's Europe, Export Marketing* and *Executive Companion*.

The Reviewer

Alex Roney, LLB Barrister, has been the Legal Counsellor of the London Chamber of Commerce and Industry since 1973, after being one of the first stagiaires to join the European Commission from the UK.

Besides being the author of the *EC/EU Fact Book* (Kogan Page, 1995), she has contributed to and edited many other publications.

Introduction

The European Union (EU) is renowned for having its own vocabulary, the "Eurospeak" of Brussels, whose terms spill over into reference books such as *Croner's Europe* and daily newspapers which cannot help but incorporate the official language when discussing European policies.

This pocket book is aimed at defining the more common terms, directives, programmes, institutions and their abbreviations. It is hoped that it will be used in conjunction with the loose-leaf to shed light on those words which are often simply the normal working shorthand of the European Commission. However, it cannot claim to be comprehensive as new terms are coined each month, new programmes initiated and there remain many terms so specialised that they are hardly ever heard by those taking a general business interest in the workings of the EU.

How to use this book

This pocket book is not designed to be read from beginning to end, but dipped into when the reader needs a fuller explanation for an EU term found perhaps in a newspaper, journal or *Croner's Europe*. The terms defined are in alphabetical order. Many common abbreviations are cross-referenced to their full term.

A

accession   The process of a country becoming a Member State of the European Union. Member States are said to "accede" to the Treaty of Rome by signature of accession agreements.

  The term can also relate to the formal agreement to comply with the provisions of an international convention.

ACP states   African, Caribbean and Pacific countries which are associated with the EU through the Lomé Convention. Products from the 68 ACP states who are signatories to the convention have access to the EU market by way of special tariff preferences. *See also **Lomé Convention**.*

Acquired Rights Directive   Directive 77/187, also known as the Business Transfer Directive, provides that on the transfer of an undertaking or company the employment rights of the employees of the company taken over are preserved as if they had been continuously employed by the new employer. The directive has been implemented throughout the EU and protects employee rights in such circumstances. The Transfer of Undertakings (Protection of Employment) Regulations 1981 (TUPE) implement these provisions in the UK. *See also **transfer of undertakings**.*

acquis communautaire   The acceptance of the obligations of EU membership by current Member States, new members and the members of the European Economic Area.

administrative letter   *See **comfort letter**.*

advertising   *See **misleading advertising**.*

adoption   Final and formal approval of proposed EU legislation by the Council of Ministers. The term may also refer to approval of legislation at its earlier stages by the European Commission.

advisory committee   A committee set up to provide advice to the European Commission in a number of areas, for example in relation to particular agricultural produce. Also known as a consultative committee.

Advocate General   An official of the European Court of Justice (ECJ) whose role includes preparing a detailed legal opinion on cases presented to the court. The ECJ usually follows this opinion in its subsequent judgment. There is, however, no legal obligation on the ECJ to follow the opinion which is made publicly available. Often the opinion contains much more detailed legal reasoning than will be found in the final court decision.

agent   Person or firm acting on behalf of another. *See also **Commercial Agents Directive**.*

agreement   A written or oral agreement or non-binding understanding between undertakings, ie businesses. An agreement may exist even where a supplier sends a unilateral letter to distributors which then forms part of the agreement. Competition rules apply to agreements even where restrictions are included in the agreement which infringe Article 85 of the Treaty of Rome.

ancillary restraint   A restriction which is subsidiary to another, ie not the main provision of an agreement. For example, under the EU merger rules there is a notice setting the time limit and the terms permitted for ancillary restrictions in relation to mergers.

anti-competitive agreement   An agreement which distorts competition within the Single Market. Article 85 of the Treaty of Rome prohibits anti-competitive agreements and agreements having equivalent effect on trade between EU Member States. Many categories of agreement have been found to infringe the competition rules, including cartels, market sharing and price fixing agreements; less obvious infringements are information exchange agreements and restrictions in relation to patent and know-how licensing which may be subject to block exemption provisions.

anti-dumping   *See dumping.*

anti-trust   Another term for competition law, used primarily in the USA. *See also competition law.*

applicable law   The national law which applies to a particular transaction or agreement. Many countries are signatories of the Rome Convention on the Law Applicable to Contractual Obligation 1980, drafted by the EU, which provides that the parties' choice of national law will be respected. Similarly, the Convention on the Law Applicable to Contracts for the International Sale of Goods, signed at the Hague in 1985, specified that the law which applies to a sale of goods contract is that named expressly by the parties. If no law is stated as having been chosen to apply to a particular agreement, the country's laws with the closest connection with the contract will apply. The national law applicable to an agreement may in theory be different from the court which has jurisdiction.

approximation   The process of bringing national laws closer where more precise harmonisation is not desired or possible, so that national differences are reduced, though not entirely removed. *See also harmonisation.*

arbitration   A process by which disputes may be settled without the parties going through the courts. Many cross-border agreements provide for international arbitration under the rules of bodies such as the International Chamber of Commerce, with the arbitration to be held in, for example, Paris or Geneva. However, arbitration can be more time-consuming and expensive than litigation and there may be no right of appeal.

article   A provision in an EU treaty which in English statutes would be called a "section".

Articles 30–36   *See free movement of goods.*

Article 85   The provision in the Treaty of Rome which prohibits anti-competitive agreements which restrict, prevent or distort competition in the EU. This article applies directly in all Member States and is often used against cartels. Infringement of Article 85 results in clauses in agreements being void and unenforceable, may result in fines of up to 10% of annual worldwide turnover and gives third parties the right to bring actions for damages. The article only applies where the ·agreement affects trade between Member States.

Article 86   The provision in the Treaty of Rome which prohibits abuses of a dominant position by businesses in the EU. Examples of breaches of this article include: refusing to supply an existing customer, for example, where they have begun to operate in competition with the dominant company, selectively reducing prices to stop competition (known as predatory pricing), unfair or excessive prices, tying clauses, and refusal to license intellectual property rights. Article 86 prohibits such conduct only where a business is "dominant", which usually means where it enjoys a market share of 40% or more in the EU or a substantial part thereof. The rules apply only where the conduct affects trade between Member States.

Article 90   A provision of the Treaty of Rome which applies to state bodies who are given special rights such as a monopoly over gas or transport. In this way state-owned bodies such as postal organisations are subject to the EC competition rules.

Article 118   The provision of the Treaty of Rome which gives the Commission the task of promoting close co-operation between Member States in the social field, particularly in relation to:
- employment law
- labour law and working conditions
- basic and advanced vocational training
- social security
- prevention of occupational accidents and diseases
- occupational hygiene
- the right of association and collective bargaining between employers and workers.

Article 177 A provision of the Treaty of Rome allowing questions of European law which arise in cases before national courts to be referred to the European Court of Justice (ECJ) before returning to the national court for a final judgment. It gives the ECJ jurisdiction to give preliminary rulings on the interpretation of the Treaty of Rome and the validity and interpretation of acts of the institutions of the EU.

assent procedure The procedure introduced by the Single European Act 1986 whereby following a Council common position on a new legislative measure, the European Parliament, at a single meeting, either approves or does not approve the common position. This may be done by a simple or absolute majority depending on the subject matter of the legislation.

association agreement An agreement with a non-EU country as provided for in Article 238 of the Treaty of Rome. The agreement may be with a country or a union of states or even an international organisation and establishes in each case an association involving reciprocal rights and obligations, common action and special procedures. The European Parliament has a right of veto over proposed new association agreements. Many countries which become Member States of the EU begin the process by means of an association agreement.

asylum A right of refuge in one country because of persecution or economic distress in another. The right of asylum protects the human rights of economic refugees and is the subject of a convention between the Member States. The Maastricht Treaty provides that on the initiative of any Member State or the Commission, asylum policy may come under qualified majority voting in the Council of Ministers. The Council is empowered to determine the third countries whose nationals must be in possession of a visa when entering the EU.

atypical workers A term used by the European Commission to mean workers such as temporary workers, part-time workers and employees engaged on a fixed-term contract, as distinguished from full-time workers. Directives have been proposed in areas such as working hours, training and social security in relation to such workers. In *R v Secretary of State ex parte*

Seymour–Smith and another [1995] IRLR 464, it was held that the UK's policy of not giving the same rights to claim unfair dismissal to workers who work part-time as those who work full-time is discriminatory on the grounds of sex because more women work part-time. The UK must change the law in this field.

B

barrier   A term used by the European Commission to describe an obstacle preventing the operation of the Single Market. The treaties establishing the EU aim to remove technical, fiscal and physical barriers between the Member States.

BC-NET   *See Business Co-operation Network.*

Benelux   Collective term for Belgium, the Netherlands and Luxembourg which co-operate closely in a number of areas. These countries signed a treaty at the Hague in 1958 to formalise such co-operation. They have harmonised their legal regimes in a number of areas, including intellectual property rights.

Berne Convention   First signed in 1886 this convention establishing the International Union for the Protection of Literary and Artistic Works (Berne Union) has been revised five times. It provides for reciprocal protection for works of citizens of countries acceding to the convention provided publication takes place in a Berne Union country. All Member States of the EU are members.

BEUC   *See European Bureau of Consumers' Unions.*

biotechnology   The manipulation of biological processes for industrial purposes. Biotechnological inventions will be the subject of harmonised legislative protection under proposals for an EU directive in this field, which will protect such inventions by patent. In 1995 a proposed directive was rejected at the final stage by the European Parliament, but in 1996 a new draft was prepared. Whether this is adopted or not, the European

Patent Office has built up a body of case law concerning when a biotechnological invention will be patentable.

black-listed clause A provision in a commercial agreement which has been held by the European Commission under a competition law regulation to infringe Article 85 of the Treaty of Rome. The EC competition rules in Article 85 of the Treaty of Rome prohibit anti-competitive agreements, but by general regulations exempt certain types of agreement. Such exemption regulations typically list clauses which are banned in such contracts — known as the "black list" in the regulation. Clauses on the black list will infringe the competition rules and thus be void.

block exemption Sometimes known as a group exemption, block exemptions are regulations which have direct effect in the Member States and which provide for an exemption from Article 85 of the Treaty of Rome for certain types of anti-competitive agreements. Block exemptions exist in a number of different areas including exclusive distribution and purchasing agreements, motor vehicle distribution, franchising, research and development, and specialisation agreements and technology transfer agreements. The regulations are published in the Official Journal of the European Community.

Brussels Convention The Convention on Jurisdiction and the Enforcement of Judgments in Civil and Commercial Matters that details which courts will have jurisdiction in relation to international disputes. All EU states are individually a party to the convention, including the UK. Generally, if a contract provides that a certain country's courts will hear any disputes which arise, this will be respected. The convention also provides rules governing circumstances where the parties have not chosen a forum for their disputes. *See also **Lugano Convention**.*

Brussels, Treaty of The treaty signed in 1992 concerning the accession of Denmark, Ireland and the UK to the then European Economic Community.

budget The annual budget of the European Union to which Member States are obliged to contribute. The Commission prepares a draft budget which is sent to the Council of Ministers which can adopt it or amend it by a qualified majority. It then goes to the European Parliament which can adopt it or propose amendments. The budget is then re-examined by the Council which can accept it or amend it again, then it goes to the European Parliament for a second reading where it will be accepted or rejected.

The amounts contributed by Member States to the budget depend on their gross national product (GNP). Some states are net contributors, in other words they pay out more than they gain. There are regular disputes over the levels of certain Member States' contributions.

Bulletin of the EU A publication issued 11 times a year describing the activities of the Commission.

Business Co-operation Network (BC–NET) A central database of companies seeking partners for financial, technical or commercial purposes. It is administered by EU staff in Brussels but a network of over 600 advisors, based in all the Member States at bodies such as Euro Info Centres, act as correspondents. To maintain confidentiality, the names of those searching for a partner are not revealed to prospective partners.

Business Transfer Directive *See **Acquired Rights Directive.***

C

cabotage   The collection and delivery of goods inside one country by hauliers from another. Article 75 of the Treaty of Rome provides that the Council of Ministers may determine when non-resident carriers may operate transport services within a Member State.

CADDIA   Co-operation in Automation of Data and Documentation. This is a European programme which provides for information exchange in relation to the customs union, agricultural area and statistical data on community trade.

CAP   *See **Common Agricultural Policy**.*

cartel   An anti-competitive agreement usually between competitors as to the prices or terms on which they will each supply their customers or dividing available work between themselves by price fixing and market sharing. Such practices are contrary to Article 85 of the Treaty of Rome and can be punished by fines of up to 10% of the annual worldwide turnover of offending businesses. Fines of millions of ECUs are not uncommon in this area. The competition rules are policed by DG IV of the European Commission. *See also **Article 85**.*

Cassis de Dijon   A leading case of 1979 in which the European Court of Justice held that products marketed legally in one Member State could not be barred from importation by another Member State because they do not conform to the requirements of the importing country's own technical or commercial standards. National regulations must not interfere with such freedom to market throughout the EU. *See also **mutual recognition**.*

Ceccini Report   A major study commissioned by the EU and published in 1988 by Paulo Ceccini about the benefits of the Single Market. It set out the costs of retaining a divided market and stressed the economic gains of the internal market.

CEDEFOP   *See **European Centre for the Development of Vocational Training**.*

CELEX   A database of EU material of a legislative nature, including directives, regulations and treaties, plus national legislation.

CE marking   Applying "CE" in a prescribed form to certain products to indicate that they have complied with particular EU directives, for example machinery, toys and electro-magnetic compatibility goods may be marked in this way. CE marking is not a quality mark, but indicates that health and safety and other legislation has been complied with. The manufacturer or first importer into the EU must apply the CE marking. Fines can be levied for breach of the rules.

CEN   Comité Européen de Normalisation or European Committee for Standardisation. This is the standards institute of the EU and EFTA countries. It develops EU standards and gathers information about national standards by local bodies. It works closely with the UK equivalent, the British Standards Institution (BSI).

CENELEC   Comité Européen de Normalisation Electrotechnique or the European Committee for Electrotechnical Standardisation. It works with CEN (see above) in setting standards in relation to electrical appliances and other devices in related fields.

certification   Certifying that a product conforms to various EU legislative requirements, such as is required before CE Marking (see above) can be applied to goods. Also, under the EU Trade Marks Directive (89/104), a "certification" trade mark must be available in the Member States. This is a mark issued by a trade association or other body which members may apply to goods or services of a stated type where they comply with certain rules.

Cockfield, Lord   Regarded as the architect of the Single European Market, the Commissioner who drew up the 1985 White Paper on Completing the Single Market. As a result of this White Paper, a programme of 282 directives to be agreed by 31 December 1992 was established.

co-decision procedure   One of several alternative procedures which may be used to pass legislation through the various EU institutions. It was introduced by the Maastricht Treaty and is sometimes called the New Co-operation Procedure. It provides for a third reading by the European Parliament requiring a simple majority to support common positions reached by the Council of Ministers. It also allows the Parliament to reject proposals in some areas.

Code Napoléon   The civil code legal system adopted across much of continental Europe. This is very different from the Anglo-Saxon common law legal system which is based on case law. The Code Napoléon consists of a commercial code setting out in a statute the rights and obligations of businesses and individuals in particular situations. It leads to much shorter legal contracts because the parties' rights are enshrined in the relevant code.

cohesion   The policy of ensuring that the poorer parts of the EU are able to share in economic growth of the richer Member States by a system of grants and funds which are directed to support less developed regions.

COM Document   A publication containing the early stage of a legislative proposal. Issued by the European Commission, such documents are identified by their reference numbers, eg COM (96) 123. The Commission often solicits views on proposals set out in a COM Document. COM Documents can be obtained from the Commission and are increasingly being made available on the Internet. They can also be purchased from HMSO in the UK.

comfort letter   A letter written by the Competition Directorate (DG IV) of the Commission stating that no action will be taken following a notification for exemption or negative clearance of an agreement which may infringe the EC competition rules (*see **Article 85***). Such a letter has no binding force and may be an informal or a formal letter. It would be unusual for the Commission to fine a business in relation to an agreement which was notified and in relation to which a comfort letter was then issued.

When making a notification the parties are asked if they would be prepared to accept a comfort letter. Most do so as this is quicker than a formal decision, however, the process is still likely to take a year or more.

Commercial Agents Directive   Directive 86/653 under which agents are given significant legal protection akin to that offered to employees. The directive harmonises agency law throughout the EU but does not apply to all agents, only those who sell goods, not services. The directive does not apply to distributors who buy and sell goods on their own account.

Commission   *See **European Commission**.*

Commissioner   A civil servant who has responsibility for a particular area of Commission policy. Commissioners serve a four year term and their appointment has to be approved by the European Parliament who may refuse or dismiss the Commission as a whole, ie not individual members. Only nationals of Member States may be members of the Commission. Commissioners must be independent in the course of their duties and not seek or take instructions from any government or other body. Members of the Commission are not permitted to engage in any other occupation, gainful or otherwise, whilst employed as a Commissioner.

Committee of Permanent Representatives (COREPER)   The body which assists the work of ministers and helps to prepare meetings and decisions of the Council of Ministers. It is made up of ambassadors to the EU and their deputies assisted by national civil servants who meet representatives of the Commission on a regular basis.

Committee of the Regions   An advisory committee established by the Maastricht Treaty. It comprises 189 members appointed by the Council of Ministers. The committee must be consulted on legislative provisions under Articles 126, 128, 129, 129(d), 130(b), 130(c) and 130(d) of the

Treaty of Rome, as amended. In practice, the committee has been consulted on a broader range of issues. The Council is allowed to impose time limits of not less than one month by which time the committee must give its opinion.

Common Agricultural Policy (CAP)   The EU policy on agriculture set out in Articles 38–43 of the Treaty of Rome. Article 39 sets out the aims of the CAP which is the increase of agricultural productivity to ensure a fair standard of living for the agricultural community, to stabilise markets, assure the availability of supplies and ensure that supplies reach consumers at a reasonable price. The treaty is supplemented by a wide range of directives in this field.

Common Customs Tariff (CCT)   The tariff which applies to imports from non-EU countries. All payments go towards the EU budget. Trade would be distorted if Member States each set their own import duties on products coming from outside the EU.

Common Foreign and Security Policy (CFSP)   Agreed at Maastricht in 1992 this provides for co-operation between Member States in matters such as foreign policy and security.

Common Market   The single European market without barriers to trade. The setting up of the Common Market was the principal purpose of the Treaty of Rome, ie to provide a free trade area. Many provisions of the treaty refer to the Common Market as do some EU regulations, though in general parlance the term EU or EC is usually used.

common position   A provisional agreement on draft EU legislation reached by the Council of Ministers after it has been examined by the European Parliament and others and possibly amended. At this stage it is published in the Official Journal of the European Communities. However, subsequent amendments may be made when the measure goes before the European Parliament again, thus a common position, whilst it is a legislative milestone with any new EU legislation, is not a final text.

Community   See **European Community (EC)**.

Community dimension   Any policy or issue which could have implications for the EU or its members.

Also, a term used in the context of EU mergers law to describe firms which have a combined worldwide turnover of more than 500 million ECU and a Community-wide turnover of at least 250 million ECU. A merger which has a Community dimension must be notified to the Merger Secretariat before it proceeds or the parties may incur significant penalties. However, no merger comes within the regulation where each of the parties derives two thirds of its EU business in one and the same Member State.

Community patent   A proposal for a patent right which would apply throughout the whole EU. Such a patent does not yet exist and should not be confused with a European patent. *See also* ***European patent***.

Community Support Framework (CSF)   Guidelines issued by the Commission for the use of structural funds for a state or region. *See also* ***structural funds***.

Community trade mark (CTM)   An EU-wide trade mark right which can be obtained by application to national trade mark offices or the Community Trade Mark Office at Alicante, Spain. The European Commission adopted the Regulation for the Community Trade Mark, Regulation 40/94, on 20 December 1993 (OJ 1994 L11). A second regulation implemented the system. The official languages of the Community trade mark are English, French, German, Italian and Spanish.

The Community Trade Mark Office opened for business on 1 April 1996 although it began accepting applications from 1 January 1996. The filing fee is 975 ECU (£800) for three classes of goods and services, and the registration fee will be 1100 ECU. Additional classes are 200 ECU each. Appealing against an adverse decision costs 800 ECU, cancellations cost 700 ECU and the 10 year renewal fee will be 2500 ECU. Marks are registered for a period of ten years and may be renewed on payment of fees.

company law   EU directives intended to harmonise corporate law throughout the EU. Directives in this area arise from articles such as Article 54.3(g) of the Treaty of Rome which provides that the Member States should co-ordinate safeguards for the protection of the interests of shareholders and others and Article 58 which provides that companies or firms formed in one Member State shall be treated in the same way as nationals of that Member State.

competence   The legal powers to handle a particular matter. For example, the European Court of Justice has competence to handle references from the national courts under Article 177 of the Treaty of Rome.

competition law   Legislation prohibiting anti-competitive agreements and abuse of a dominant position. Articles 85 and 86 of the Treaty of Rome comprise the EU competition rules which apply throughout the EU. However, various regulations exist which exempt certain categories of agreement from these rules. Breach of competition rules renders restrictions in agreements void and can result in EU fines of up to 10% of annual worldwide group turnover.

concentration   A merger of two or more companies which may need to be cleared in advance by the European Commission under the EU competition rules.

concerted practice   An activity which may affect trade between Member States by the prevention, restriction or distortion of competition. A concerted practice will not be a formal written agreement, but instead an activity undertaken by several businesses which has an anti-competitive effect. Article 85 of the Treaty of Rome prohibits concerted practices.

conciliation procedure   One of several alternative methods for the adoption of an EU directive. This was inserted into the Treaty of Rome by Article 189b of the Maastricht Treaty. It can be used for adoption of directives plus a wide range of other matters, such as:
- legislation on freedom of movement for workers
- directives on freedom of establishment
- approximation of laws
- incentive measures relating to education and public health

- action supporting Member States' policies to protect consumers
- guidelines in relation to trans-European networks for transport, tele-communications and energy infrastructures
- multi-annual framework programmes on research and technological development
- general action programmes setting out priority objectives to be attained in an environmental policy.

The procedure is very similar to that of the co-operation procedure. However, where Parliament accepts the measure or takes no action within three months of receiving the Council of Ministers' common position at second reading, the Council will adopt the measure in question as set out in the common position. If Parliament does not propose to adopt the measure as it stands then it meets with the Conciliation Committee and it has the option to reject the common position altogether.

consultative document   A document circulated by the Commission to EU advisory committees and bodies before a formal proposal for new legislation is issued.

consultation procedure   A procedure for compulsory consultation before EU measures are adopted. It was last altered by the Maastricht Treaty. Parliament must be consulted in areas such as the voting rights of nationals of Member States in local and European elections, state aid regulations, agreements on the exchange rate system, research and technological development programmes and international agreements. Parliament can also oblige the Council of Ministers to consult it again where a proposal is subsequently modified.

consumer protection   An area of law harmonised by several EU directives. Legislation includes the Product Liability Directive (85/374), General Product Safety Directive (92/590), Directive on Contracts Negotiated Away from Business Premises (85/577) and the Unfair Terms in Consumer Contracts Directive (93/13).

convention   An international agreement to which different nation states or international bodies may accede, under which the participants agree to abide by the tenets of the convention.

convergence criteria   The criteria laid down by the Maastricht Treaty which are required to be satisfied before individual Member States are permitted to move towards economic and monetary union by means of the single European currency. Certain financial targets must first be met, as laid down in the Protocol on the Convergence Criteria referred to in Article 109j of the Maastricht Treaty:

(a)   an average rate of inflation, observed over a year, which does not exceed by more than 1.5% the average inflation rate of the three best performing Member States

(b)   the avoidance of excessive government budget deficit, which is defined as meaning an annual budget deficit of less than 3% of Gross Domestic Product (GDP) and an overall public debt ratio not exceeding 60% of GDP

(c)   the Member State's currency must have been in the narrow 2.5% band of the exchange rate mecanism of the European Monetary System without severe tensions for at least two years

(d)   the Member State's average long-term interest rate, measured over a period of one year before examination, does not exceed by more than 2% of the average interest rates in the three best performing states in terms of price stability.

co-operation agreement   An agreement between independent companies or businesses of mutual co-operation in relation to certain matters. The EU has issued a notice on co-operation agreements which sets out how various forms of co-operation are permitted under the EU competition rules. These should not be confused with the trade and co–operation agreements between the EU and third countries.

co-operation procedure   A method of agreeing EU measures brought in by the Single European Act 1986. The procedure is similar to the consultation procedure but there are no time limits on Parliament to give its opinion at the first reading stage. Once Parliament has given its opinion the Council may adopt a common position, again without a time limit. Once the measure is at second reading stage, if the Parliament has no amendments, it is adopted as set out in the common position. Many of the areas of legislation to which this procedure originally applied were subsequently moved to the conciliation procedure by the Maastricht Treaty.

Copyright Term Directive   Directive 93/98 which requires all Member States to harmonise the length of protection of copyright works to the life of the author plus 70 years. (This was previously life plus 50 years in the UK.) The directive has resulted in works out of copyright coming back into protection in some Member States.

COREPER   *See **Committee of Permanent Representatives**.*

Council of Europe   An organisation created at the end of the Second World War to promote European unity and protect human rights. There are 31 members including all EU Member States. The assembly of the Council of Europe elects the judges of the European Court of Human Rights. The Council of Europe has concluded about 130 inter-governmental conventions and agreements. It should not be confused with the Council of Ministers of the EU.

Council of the European Union   *See **Council of Ministers**.*

Council of Ministers   Otherwise known as the Council of the European Union, this body guards the interests of the Member States and consists of government ministers from each Member State. The ministers change according to the nature of the matter, for example, transport ministers from each country would meet to discuss matters relating to transport. Heads of government meet at a "summit" two or three times a year to discuss major issues and chart the future course of the EU. The Council of Ministers adopts decisions, regulations and directives and is an important part of the EU legislative process.

counterfeit control   Legislative measures to stop pirated or copied products being distributed in breach of the intellectual rights of the owners. The EU agreed regulation 3295/94 giving customs officers powers to seize products at borders which infringe trade marks and copyright. This was implemented in the UK on 1 July 1995 by SI 1995/1445.

countervailing duties   Fees which are ordered to be paid to ameliorate the effects of "dumping" products on the EU market. They are required to be paid by the business which was responsible for the dumping. *See also dumping*.

Court of Auditors   An institution of the EU whose function it is to check the accounts of all EU institutions to ensure that money has been received and expenditure has been incurred in accordance with the law. It monitors the budget and "off-budget" activities and reports annually.

Court of First Instance (CFI)   The first appeal court for decisions of the European Commission in matters such as competition law and staffing disputes within the Commission, ie direct actions brought by natural or legal persons. From the CFI appeals may be made to the European Court of Justice (ECJ). It was set up to relieve the burden on the ECJ but does not deal with actions brought by Members States.

Court of Justice   *See European Court of Justice (ECJ).*

customs code   A code to establish and consolidate on an EU-wide basis customs rules within the Single Market. Regulation 2913/92 established the customs code. The term is also used for a special numbering system under which all goods sold in the EU are given a code. The code is then used to determine customs duties which are paid on importation into the EU.

customs union   A single customs territory without barriers to trade, whether in the EU or elsewhere.

D

damages   Money which is part of an out of court settlement or ordered by a court to be paid as compensation. For example, under EU competition law those who suffer loss through the operation of an agreement contrary to Article 85 or an abusive practice contrary to Article 86 are entitled to sue the perpetrator of such practices for damages in the national courts. Damages will compensate the victim of a cartel for the loss which they have suffered, but it can be difficult to prove that a loss flowed from a particular activity; so such actions are not common. The European Commission is keen to encourage actions in the national courts and issued a notice regarding this on 23 December 1992.

Damages may also be claimed from a national government for failure to implement a directive at all, on time or improperly where there is a clear and substantial failure. Such damages can run into millions of pounds.

Database Directive   Directive 96/9 (published at OJ 1996 L77/20) on the legal protection of databases which provides that Member States must protect databases by copyright. A database is defined as a collection of independent works, data or other materials arranged in a systematic or methodical way and individually accessible by electronic or other means. Those databases protected are those which are seen to constitute the author's own intellectual creation because of the way the contents have been arranged or selected. This is a separate protection from the contents of the database which may be protected by copyright on its own account. Member States have until 1 January 1998 to implement the directive. The directive also provides that databases which do not meet these standards may instead be entitled to lesser protection, ie a right to prevent unfair extraction is given.

data protection   The protection of individuals' rights in personal data. The EU has agreed the Data Protection Directive 95/46 (published at OJ 1995 L281/31) which harmonises protection of data throughout the EU and requires that all data about individuals must be held, obtained and used in accordance with certain rules. There is compulsory registration for those holding data of this type whether on computer or in non-electronic or other form. Each Member State must appoint a data protection officer entrusted with enforcement of the legislation.

dawn raid   Entry of premises by European Commission officials to obtain further evidence of illegal cartels or abuses of a dominant position contrary to EU competition law. Regulation 17/62 gives the Commission power to make such raids which can be without notice to the parties. Commission officials have a right to look through filing cabinets, computer systems and even desks and personal briefcases, but cannot take documents which are protected by "privilege", ie correspondence between external lawyers and their clients. Entry of such officials must not be refused and reception staff and security officers should be left general instructions as to what to do if Commission officials arrive. Despite their name, the raids are usually carried out during normal working hours and Commission officials from Brussels will usually be accompanied by officials from the national competition authority, for example in the UK, the Office of Fair Trading.

decision   An act of the European Commission which is binding on an individual, a legal entity such as a business or the Member States. The Court of First Instance and European Court of Justice also issue decisions.

declaration of origin   A statement of the origin of goods for export which is applied to the goods by the supplier, manufacturer or exporter. This may appear on the invoice or any other document relating to the goods. A certificate of origin proves from where goods came. National laws requiring businesses to mark the origin of goods from within the EU may infringe Article 30 of the Treaty of Rome.

decompilation   The taking apart of computer software, otherwise known as reverse engineering. Under the Software Directive 91/250 (published at OJ 1991 L122/42 as amended by 93/98 OJ 1993 L290/9) computer software is protected by copyright throughout the EU. However, a very limited right to decompilation is given in that directive for a defined permitted purpose, ie to write an interoperable program. Any attempt by contract to exclude this limited right will be void.

Definitive VAT Regime   A value added tax system (VAT) within the EU which is due to come into force on 1 January 1997. *See* **origin system.**

delegation   The passing on of responsibility for action or enforcement to others. The Treaty of Rome empowers the Council of Ministers to delegate its powers to the Commission.

Delors, Jaques   President of the EU from 1985 to 1992 who did much to help achieve the Single Market.

de minimis   A limit, usually financial, below which certain rules will not apply because of minimal impact.

deregulation   A movement at EU level to cut back rules which are not needed or which could be better set at national level. *See also* **subsidiarity.**

derogation   An exemption clause which permits a Member State to avoid a certain directive, regulation or action in a policy area. Sometimes one Member State is given longer than another to implement an EU directive, eg the Commercial Agents Directive (86/653) had to be implemented by 1990 by most Member States, but other countries such as the UK and Eire had extended deadlines.

destination system   The system whereby value added tax (VAT) is collected in the country where the goods are sold which is their "destination" and not where they are made. This system is likely to continue until at least 1 January 1997 when it is hoped that Member States will move to the origin system, otherwise known as the final, or definitive VAT regime. *See also* **origin system.**

direct effect   A term used to describe EU measures which apply in Member States without the requirement for national implementing legislation. Regulations and provisions of the Treaty of Rome have direct effect in Member States. Directives generally must be implemented by way of national laws.

directive   A piece of EU legislation, usually designed to harmonise the law in a particular area. Directives are aimed at Member States which must then implement them into national law, usually within two to three years of the date of the directive. In the UK this will be by way of a statutory instrument or an Act of Parliament. Directives are published in the Official Journal of the European Communities.

Directorate General (DG)   A separate division within the Commission having responsibility for a particular policy area. For a list of DGs and their responsibilities, see page 2–5 of Volume One, *Croner's Europe*.

direct taxation   Taxation of income rather than expenditure. There is no harmonisation of personal income tax at EU level. However, there have been measures on company taxation, such as the Directive on Parents and Subsidiaries (90/435) which provides for a common system of taxation applicable to parents and subsidiaries of different Member States. Taxation applicable to mergers, divisions, transfer of assets and exchanges of shares concerning companies of different Member States was dealt with by Directive 90/434.

disabled workers   Workers with mental or physical disabilities. There are various EU programmes designed to improve the position of the disabled in the workforce.

discrimination   *See* **racism** *and* **sex discrimination**.

distribution regulation   An EU regulation setting out what provisions may be included in an exclusive distibution agreement in order to comply with the competition rules. Separate regulations on exclusive purchasing, motor vehicle distribution and franchising have also been agreed. These regulations should be followed in drafting agreements for the distribution of goods within the EU in order to avoid a breach of Article 85 of the Treaty of Rome.

domicile   A place of residence or permanent abode, defined more precisely in much tax and nationality legislation throughout the EU. Freedom of movement of workers in the Community is guaranteed under EU law and no discrimination must be exercised by employers as to EU workers' nationality or domicile.

dominant position   A term used to describe a business which is able to act without having too much regard to the actions of its competitors. Often this will be the case where it enjoys a market share of 40% or more in a particular product market. The dominant position exists where it is enjoyed over the whole EU or a substantial part thereof, which may comprise one large country, such as the UK or a larger part of the EU if the country is small, such as Luxembourg. Article 86 of the Treaty of Rome prohibits an abuse of a dominant position but does not define it.

Doorstep Selling Directive   Common term for the Directive on Contracts Negotiated Away from Business Premises (85/577) that requires that contracts made away from business premises must be subject to a right for the consumer to cancel the contract. Member States are obliged to enact this into their national law.

draft   An early stage of EU legislation. For new legislation there is usally a preliminary consultation by way of a Green Paper. Comments are considered and draft directives or regulations are then formulated.

drivers' controls   Limits on the number of hours at a stretch which commercial drivers may spend at the wheel. These are enshrined in EU legislation, which also specifies the breaks they must take for rest and sleep on long journeys and requires tachographs to be carried and used in cabs.

dual pricing   A system of two prices for agricultural produce operated in the EU under the Common Agricultural Policy (CAP). The CAP supports the food price whereas goods imported are subject to import levies. EU-grown produce sold outside the EU is often sold at a lower price and may be subsidised by the EU.

dumping   The placing of low-priced goods on the EU market by companies in third countries. EU dumping regulations prohibit the sale of goods at below normal value. There may be transitional periods during which such regulations do not apply, eg after a new member joins the EU. Counter-vailing duties may be ordered on goods which are dumped to remove the effects of the illegal dumping. These are also known as anti-dumping duties.

duty free goods   Goods purchased within the EU by EU nationals in coun-tries other than that of their residence which may be imported into other EU states without payment of customs' duties. Such goods must be intended for personal use and not resale. Duty free zones operate at airports and similar places.

E

EAGGF   *See **European Agricultural Guidance and Guarantee Fund.***

Eastern Europe   Collective term usually referring to former Communist countries which were part of the Soviet Bloc, many of which now wish to join the EU. These include the Czech Republic, Slovakia, Romania, Hungary, Bulgaria, Poland and the former Yugoslavia.

EBRD   *See **European Bank for Reconstruction and Development.***

EC   *See **European Community.***

ECHO   *See **European Commission Host Organisation.***

ECJ   *See **European Court of Justice.***

Ecolabel   An EU designation with logo to be used where products comply with environmental requirements in particular directives. Ecolabels were first available for washing machines and dishwashers. Manufacturers in those areas whose products meet the standards required in the relevant directive may apply the ecolabel to their products and consumers will then know that these products when used will provide less damage to the environment than some products without this label.

Economic and Monetary Union (EMU)   The political goal of creating a common monetary policy and a common currency for the EU. The third stage of monetary union envisaged in the Maastricht Treaty is a single currency to be introduced no later than 1 January 1999. Convergence criteria must be met before EMU is possible for individual Member States. *See also **convergence criteria.***

Economic and Social Committee (ESC, ECOSOC)   An advisory body made up of representatives of trade and industry which represents various economic sectors and interests and is divided into different opinion groups. It must be consulted on proposals for legislation in certain policy areas.

ECSC   *See European Coal and Steel Community.*

ECU   *See European Currency Unit.*

EDC   *See European Documentation Centre.*

EEA   *See European Economic Area.*

EEC   *See European Community.*

EFTA   *See European Free Trade Area.*

EFTA Surveillance Authority   Known also as ESA, this body has a similar function in connection with Norway, Iceland and Liechtenstein as the European Commission has in relation to the Member States of the EU: it is a body of civil servants which regulates compliance with the rules of the European Economic Area Agreement. There are complicated rules setting out when the provisions of the Treaty of Rome will apply to particular transactions and when the EEA agreement's provisions will apply. The EFTA Surveillance Authority, like the Commission, has powers to carry out investigations into breaches of the rules and to make decisions and impose fines for breaches of the EEA competition rules which are very similar to Article 85 and 86 of the Treaty of Rome.

EHLASS   *See European Home and Leisure Accidents Surveillance System.*

EIC   *See Euro Info Centre.*

electro-magnetic compatibility   An area of legislation which requires those producing electronic devices to ensure that such devices do not interfere with other similar devices. These rules are set out in an Electro-Magnetic Compatibility Directive (89/332) as amended by Directive 92/31. The directive was implemented in the UK by SI 1992/2372 as amended by SI 1994/3080 on 1 January 1996. It applies to apparatus liable to cause electromagnetic disturbance or the performance of which is liable to be affected by such disturbance. Apparatus is defined as an electrical or electronic appliance or system consisting of a finished product or products which has an intrinsic function which is intended for the end user and is supplied as a single commercial unit. Guidance notes on these requirements have been issued by the DTI. Infringement of the rules in the UK can lead to a fine of up to £5000 and/or three months in jail.

EMS See *European Monetary System.*

EMU See *Economic and Monetary Union.*

EN See *Euro Norm.*

enlargement The process of enlarging the EU by means of increasing membership. Countries which have applied to become Member States include Turkey, Malta and many eastern European states.

ERM See *Exchange Rate Mechanism.*

EP See *European Parliament.*

EPC See *European Patent Convention.*

equal oppportunities EU law requires that men and women be treated equally. Article 119 of the Treaty of Rome provides that men and women receive equal pay for equal work. In the UK this legislation is contained in the Sex Discrimination Act 1975 and the Equal Pay Act 1970. The EU encourages equal opportunities for men and women and references can be made to the European Court of Justice where national law does not appear to comply with EU law in this field.

equal treatment The principle of the free movement of workers throughout the EU whatever their Member State nationality as enshrined in Articles 48–50 of the Treaty of Rome. Nationals of one Member State moving to another must be treated equally with those from the state to which they have moved. There should be no discrimination in relation to pay, social security and tax benefits.

ESC   *See **Economic and Social Committee**.*

ETSI   *See **European Telecommunications Standards Institute**.*

EU   *See **European Union**.*

EURATOM   *See **European Atomic Energy Community**.*

euro   The proposed single European currency.

EUROCOOP   *See **European Community of Consumer Co-operatives**.*

Eurocontrol   *See **European Organisation for the Safety of Air Navigation**.*

Euro Info Centre (EIC)   The network of EICs was set up by the European Commission to provide information to members of the public and businesses about EU matters. EICs can be found across all the Member States.

Euro norm (EN)   A European standard adopted by CEN and CENELEC in place of a national standard. Many EU directives require that products conform to a relevant EN if one exists. Where a relevant EN does not exist, products may be required to conform to equivalent national or international standards.

Europe Agreement   An association agreement entered into by the EU and countries of Eastern and Central Europe such as Bulgaria, Romania, the Baltic states and Lithuania.

European Agricultural Guidance and Guarantee Fund (EAGGF, FEOGA)
A fund which aims to increase productivity of agriculture through technical progress and best use of production facilities as well as necessary modernisation of agricultural infrastructures. The guarantee part of this fund finances EU market interventions and stabilisation of agricultural markets.

European Atomic Energy Community (EURATOM)   One of the three original European Communities, the others being the European Economic Community under the Treaty of Rome and the European Coal and Steel Community. Euratom was established from 1 January 1958 to establish the nuclear industries and direct them to peaceful use to achieve a single energy market.

European Bank for Reconstruction and Development (EBRD) Established in 1990 this institution aims to promote the advantages of an open market economy in central and eastern Europe. The Member States of the EU own 51% of the bank's capital but it has 57 participating states in total. It can provide loans for infrastructure projects in the central and eastern European states and has its headquarters in London. Its president is Jacques de Larosiere.

European Bureau of Consumers' Unions (BEUC) A group of consumers' associations in the Member States which has established its own consumer programme.

European Central Bank (ECB) Not yet set up, this bank will be instituted to progress the third stage of economic and monetary union (*see Economic and Monetary Union (EMU)*). It is preceeded by a European Monetary Institute (EMI) set up on 1 January 1994 and comprising the governors of the national central banks and a president. By 31 December 1996 the EMI is due to specify the regulatory and other framework necessary for the ECB.

European Centre for the Development of Vocational Training (CEDEFOP) Set up in 1975, this body aims to promote and develop vocational and in-service training. It is based in Thessaloniki in Greece.

European Coal and Steel Community (ECSC) One of the three original European communities, the others being the European Economic Community and the European Atomic Energy Community. It co-ordinates policies of the Member States in the areas of coal and steel, and contains provisions similar to those of the Treaty of Rome, for example in the fields of competition law and state aids.

European Commission The administrative body of the EU. It is made up of civil servants from each of the 15 Member States and is based in Brussels, although some departments such as the statistical office are based elsewhere. It drafts and proposes new laws. It is divided into Directorates General which have responsibilities for different policy areas. Each Member State has the right to nominate one or two Commissioners. Commissioners head the various Directorates General.

Article 155 of the Treaty of Rome provides that the Commission shall ensure that the provisions of the treaty are complied with and that recommendations or opinions are delivered on matters relating to the treaty. It also provides that the Commission shall reach decisions and shape legislative measures and exercise powers conferred on it by the Council of Ministers.

European Commission Host Organisation (ECHO)   The Community host computer. An accompanying customer service database is run from Luxembourg in connection with this.

European Community (EC)   Previously the European Economic Community (EEC). Provisions of the Treaty of Rome referring to EEC were altered by the Maastricht Treaty to read "EC". To be distinguished from the EU, which is the European Union comprising the Treaty of Rome, the Common Foreign and Security Policy and other elements emanating from the Maastricht Treaty. However, for many practical purposes this distinction is often not maintained and increasingly the term EU is used in place of EC. *See also European Union.*

European Community of Consumer Co-operatives (EUROCOOP)   A group of federations and other bodies from certain EU states which are involved in the area of consumer co-operatives.

European Convention on Human Rights   A convention signed in 1950 in Rome setting out basic human rights, similar to the Geneva Convention. It is enforced in the Member States by the European Court of Human Rights which is based in Strasbourg. Cases can be brought before the court for alleged breaches of the human rights enshrined in the convention. It is separate from the EU and not connected to it.

European Court of Justice (ECJ)   The principal court for all European litigation. It is also the appeal court from decisions of the Court of First Instance. The court is based in Luxembourg but judges come from all EU jurisdictions. Before the court reaches a decision an opinion is prepared by a court official called the Advocate General. The court usually follows the opinion of the Advocate General, though this is not invariably the case.

European Currency Unit (ECU) A unit of account made up of a basket of Member States' currencies. The ECU has a value in each national currency which fluctuates. It is used by EU institutions in setting their budgets and can be used by businesses for transactions. The ECU is a unit of account rather than a unit of currency as such, though some prices are quoted in ECU by the Commission and others. The ECU is used in the exchange rate mechanism (ERM).

European Documentation Centre (EDC) Depository of EU documentation. Many ECDs exist throughout the EU and are usually situated in libraries. The centres are open to the public.

European Economic Area (EEA) A free trade area currently made up of Norway, Iceland and Liechtenstein and the 15 EU Member States . It came into being on 1 January 1994 and provided a staging post to full membership of the EU for Austria, Sweden and Finland which joined the EU on 1 January 1995. The EEA agreement contains many provisions similar to those in the Treaty of Rome and has its own institutions, such as the EFTA Court and the EFTA Surveillance Authority (ESA). It does not have a budget.

European Free Trade Area (EFTA) A free trade area established in 1960 which originally comprised Austria, Norway, Sweden, Switzerland, Finland, Iceland and Liechtenstein. Austria, Sweden and Finland are no longer in EFTA as they joined the EU on 1 January 1995. The EFTA countries operate a free trade zone and have bilateral free trade arrangements with the EU.

European Home and Leisure Accidents Surveillance System (EHLASS) An EU system to reduce and prevent accidents at home and in the course of leisure activities.

European Investment Bank (EIB) A bank which was formed by the Treaty of Rome, Title IV, Articles 129–130. The members of the bank are the

Member States of the EU and the statute for the bank was laid down as a protocol annexed to the treaty. The task of the bank is to enhance balanced and steady development of the common market in the interests of the EU. The bank operates on a non-profit making basis and grants loans and gives guarantees to facilitate the financing of the following types of projects:

(a) projects for developing less well-developed regions

(b) projects modernising businesses or developing fresh activities where they cannot be entirely financed by means available in individual Member States

(c) projects of common interest to several Member States which are of such a size or nature that they cannot be entirely financed by the various means available in the individual Member States.

European Monetary System (EMS)   The financial system in the EU, a term used to cover the exchange rate mechanism (ERM) and the European Currency Unit (ECU). It was established in March 1979 to develop closer co-operation in monetary policy in advance of liberalisation of capital movements. Directive 88/361 removed restrictions on movement of capital between people resident in the Member States, implementing Article 67 of the Treaty of Rome.

European Organisation for the Safety of Air Navigation (EUROCONTROL) A body formed by international treaty and designed to ensure safety in the air. Its offices are situated in Belgium.

European Parliament (EP)   One of the five principal institutions of the EU, the others being the European Commission, the Court of Auditors, the European Court of Justice and the Council of Ministers. The EP is, however, the only democratic institution and consists of members who are directly elected by the citizens of the Member States. The Maastricht Treaty gave the EP more powers such as a right of veto in particular areas and greater influence under the co-decision procedure for adoption of new legislation.

European Patent Convention (EPC)   A codification of patent law signed in Munich in 1973 which aims to stengthen co-operation between the states of Europe "in respect of the protection of inventions that such protection may be obtained in those states by a single procedure of the grant of patents and by the establishment of certain standard rules governing patents so granted". It does not provide for a single EU patent, but instead one application is made to the European Patent Office in Munich for a bundle of national patents in those states where a patent is require.

Signing the convention does not require Member States to bring their national patent law into line with the convention though most states have done so, including the UK.

European patent A national patent granted for several states under the European Patent Convention of 1973 which came into force in 1978. Under this it is possible to apply to the European Patent Office (or EPO) situated in Munich for a European patent to protect new inventions. Application is made for individual patents designated in particular EU states. The patent granted is not a single patent which applies throughout the EU, though there have been proposals for a true Community-wide patent (a similar concept was recently realised in relation to trade marks, see *Community trade mark*). It may be cheaper where patenting is required in several Member States to apply to the EPO rather than making individual national applications to local patent offices.

European Regional Development Fund (ERDF) This fund makes money available for regions requiring development, depressed areas, etc. It funds EU and national programmes. DG XVI is in charge of this programme.

European Social Fund (ESF) This fund is enshrined in Articles 123–128 of the Treaty of Rome and is aimed at improving employment opportunities and living standards. One of its tasks is to increase workers' geographical and occupational mobility within the EU. The fund is administered by the Commission which is assisted by a committee of representatives of governments, trade unions and employers' organisations. The fund provides grants in a number of different areas, including vocational training and resettlement allowances.

European standard *See Euro norm.*

EUROSTAT   The statistical office of the European Community situated in Luxembourg.

European Telecommunications Standards Institute (ETSI)   The body which sets standards for the telecommunications industry. It is made up of members of that industry and was established in 1988.

European Trade Union Confederation   A grouping of national trade union bodies under an EU-wide umbrella which seeks to influence policies at EU level.

European Union (EU)   The general term in common usage referring to the alliance of 15 Member States. More specifically it is the political association comprising the European Communities, the Common Foreign and Security Policy and other matters agreed in the Treaty on European Union (Maastricht Treaty). However, the Maastricht Treaty merely altered references to European Economic Community (EEC) in the Treaty of Rome to European Community (EC), not EU. The term EC is still correct where reference is made to a matter emanating from the Treaty of Rome where it is not covered by the Maastricht Treaty.

European Works Council (EWC)   A transnational, pan-European forum of employee representatives set up for the purpose of informing and consulting with group-level management.

EWC   See *European Works Council.*

Exchange Rate Mechanism (ERM)   The system intended as a precursor to full monetary union. ERM links currencies with the aim of ensuring exchange rate stability. The effect for members is that central national banks are not allowed to fluctuate their currencies more than a certain percentage above (called the ceiling rate) or below (minimum rate) a central rate which is set out in ECUs. They may need to intervene in foreign exchange markets to buy or sell currency to achieve the necessary adjustments or alter interest rates. The UK joined the ERM in 1990, but has since left, together with Greece and Italy.

excluded sectors   Sectors outside the EU public procurement regime usually for a transitional period after a Member State joins the EU.

The term also applies to low value contracts below the figures set out in the various public procurement directives. The excluded sector does not have to advertise public and utility contracts in the Official Journal of the European Communities and is not otherwise subject to the public procurement rules.

exemption   A regulation or decision removing an agreement from the provisions of the competition rules. Various EU regulations provide exemption for certain types of agreements and the Commission will grant an individual exemption under Article 85(3) where an application is made. *See also* *block exemption*.

exhaustion of rights   Once goods are placed on the market anywhere in the EU, national intellectual property rights cannot be used to prevent their importation into another EU state as the rights are said to be "exhausted". Thus geographical barriers to entry cannot be imposed. The principle is expounded in many EU cases and comes from Article 30–36 of the Treaty of Rome which prohibits quantitative restrictions on imports and all measures which have equivalent effect. For example, if "A" owns a patent in the UK and France and sells its products in the UK, it cannot sue "B" for infringement of the French patent where "B" bought the goods in the UK and imports them into France.

export ban   A clause in a contract or anti-competitive practice which has the effect of banning the resale of products outside one EU territory into another Member State. Export bans have long been held to infringe the competition rules in Article 85 of the Treaty of Rome and fines of up to 10% of annual worldwide group turnover are frequently levied by the Commission. For example, a clause preventing a distributor from selling products outside its territory would infringe the competition rules. However where the distribution exemption regulation applies it is permitted to restrict an exclusive distributor from actively soliciting sales from outside its territory.

An export ban in a written contract will be void where Article 85 applies. In addition, practices which have the effect of bolstering or imposing an export ban are forbidden, including buying up all products which have found their way into another local market, marking products solely for the purposes of tracing them to stop parallel importation of this sort and putting pressure on dealers not to engage in parallel importation.

export duties Charges levied for the export of products under various EU directives.

F

federalist Someone who believes that the European Union should develop into a grouping of federal states.

FEOGA *See European Agricultural Guidance and Guarantee Fund.*

field of use clause A clause in an agreement, usually a licence agreement, limiting the purposes to which the licensed technology may be put. Under EU competition law licensees may be restricted to exploiting licensed technology to one technical field of use, but restrictions as to their customers must not be imposed. It is not always clear as to what constitutes a field of use restriction or a customer restriction.

final VAT regime *See origin system.*

fine A financial penalty for breach of a law or a rule. For example, Regulation 17 allows the Commission to impose a fine of up to 10% of the worldwide annual group turnover of the offending company for infringements of the competition rules of the Treaty of Rome. Fines frequently run into millions of ECUs. The highest fine was 75 million ECU against Tetra Pak in July 1991. The level of fine will depend on a number of different factors including the severity of the offence and its duration, the attitude of the company during an investigation, ie whether it co-operated, and the nature of the offence. Where one company has imposed an offending agreement on another weaker party both will typically be fined, though the weaker party's fine will be less to reflect its less culpable position. The Commission has no power to fine individuals personally under the competition rules.

fiscal barrier   Tax barrier which may impede the Single Market. Although some harmonisation of taxation law has begun, most taxes are still set at national level and there are significant differences between the Member States as to the level of both business and personal taxes. This comprises a barrier to anyone wishing to start a business in an area where taxes are higher. *See also* **taxation**.

food law   EU regulations on food have resulted in harmonisation of legislation, in particular food hygiene legislation.

FORCE Initiative   An EU programme to provide continuing education for adults, including the provision of grants for teacher training.

foreign policy   Title V of the Maastricht Treaty provides that the EU will pursue a common foreign and security policy, even though this was not a part of the Treaty of Rome.

Form AB   The form required to be completed when notifying an agreement to the European Commission for an exemption or negative clearance under the competition rules. In addition to the form a complex annex with a considerable amount of information must be prepared, such as the market shares of the parties and their competitors, the relevant product market, the background to the agreement and why restrictions within it should be allowed. Form AB is updated from time to time and published in the Official Journal of the European Communities.

Form CO   The form to be completed when making a complaint to the Commission concerning breach of the competition rules. A complaint may be made without completion of the form, provided sufficient information is given to enable the Commission to take a decision as to whether the complaint has a sufficient community interest to be worth investigation.

forum shopping   Choosing the country whose laws are most favourable in which to bring a particular legal case to court. In some instances there is a choice of jurisdiction. Although the Single Market has resulted in harmonisation of laws in many areas, there are still significant national differences to make forum shopping a sensible precaution when legal action is considered. However, it is usual to provide in agreements which courts should have jurisdiction in the event of a dispute.

Fourth Framework Programme   A funding programme for technological research and development, running from 1994–98. It is designed to complement national research efforts by directing aid to projects which can only be achieved by implementation at European level.

framework directive   An umbrella directive setting out the framework within which the legislation of Member States is to be harmonised, but leaving the detail to be handled in subsequent legislation.

franchising regulation   Regulation 4087/88 of the Commission defines franchising as a package of industrial or intellectual property rights relating to trade marks, trade names, shop signs, utility models, designs, copyrights, know-how or patents, to be exploited for the resale of goods or the provision of services to end users. The franchise contract in the EU must comply with Regulation 4087/88, which sets out which provisions are permitted and which are banned under Article 85 of the Treaty of Rome.

fraud   Deception in financial matters, usually with a view to personal monetary gain. The EU aims to control fraud which in an EU context means matters such as false applications for EU grants which is particularly bad in the area of the Common Agricultural Policy.

freedom of establishment   The requirement under Article 52 of the Treaty of Rome that Member States must not restrict the rights of nationals of other Member States to establish themselves in the territory of another Member State other than on grounds such as security and health. *See also free movement of services.*

free movement of capital   Provisions enshrined in Articles 67–73 of the Treaty of Rome requiring Member States to enable capital to move freely around the EU without restrictions, in particular by ensuring that exchange controls do not apply. Directive 88/361 required Member States to abolish restrictions on the movement of capital.

free movement of goods   The principle under which goods are allowed to move freely across borders within the single European market. Articles 30–36 of the Treaty of Rome prohibit quantitative restrictions on imports and exports and all measures having equivalent effect. However, Article 36 provides that these provisions do not preclude prohibitions or restrictions justified on grounds of public morality, public policy or public security; the protection of health and life of humans, animals or plants; the protection of national treasures possessing artistic, historic or archaeological value; or the protection of industrial and commercial property.

free movement of persons   The right of EU nationals to move anywhere in the EU. Articles 48–51 of the Treaty of Rome contain this right and require that any discrimination based on nationality of workers of different Member States be abolished. Workers may move freely within the territory of Member States for the purpose of employment, stay in a Member State for this purpose and remain there after having been employed, subject to certain conditions. Whilst internal passport controls should have ceased, the UK and some other states continue to maintain border controls even for those travelling within the EU.

free movement of services   The freedom to provide services throughout the EU without let or hindrance as provided for in Articles 50–66 of the Treaty of Rome. Services include activities of an industrial or commercial character, activities of craftsmen and of the professions. The failure by one Member State to recognise a professional qualification obtained in another state prevents free movement of services and this leads to particular difficulties in those areas where standards of qualifications vary widely from country to country.

free trade   The ability to buy and sell goods and services from one state in another without regulatory or tariff restrictions. Approximately 120 trade and other agreements have been concluded between the EU and third countries, in addition to over 30 multilateral agreements.

G

GATT   *See General Agreements on Tariffs and Trade.*

General Agreements on Tariffs and Trade (GATT)   A treaty signed in 1947 to provide for a certain measure of free trade. The original aim of GATT was to reduce high tariffs on goods thereby reducing the risk of trade wars and ultimately military wars.

The latest round of GATT talks, begun in 1994 and called the Uruguay Round, led to the setting up of the World Trade Organisation (WTO). *See also **World Trade Organisation.***

Generalised System of Preferences (GSP)   Reduced tariffs for imports from some developing countries into the EU.

General Product Safety Directive   Directive 92/59 (published at OJ 1992 L228/24) which provides that products made available to consumers must be safe. The directive requires Member States to harmonise national laws and this was done in the UK by regulations (SI 1994/2328) which came into force on 3 October 1994. The directive is supplemental to the Product Liability Directive (85/374). Producers are obliged to provide information to consumers and keep themselves informed of risks a product might present and identify measures which may be taken to minimise risk. Obligations are also imposed on distributors to act with due care to ensure that these requirements are met.

genetically modified organism (GMO)   Part of a plant or animal that has been altered by a biotechnological development. Detailed EU rules exist as to the release of genetically modified organisms in order to protect the environment and public health.

geographical market A market defined geographically by area. *See also product market*.

geographical indication A system similar to trade marks known as an appellation of origin, under which 318 products are protected and their names only used for products from particular regions. The regulations were agreed in March 1996. The scheme stops others in different regions using local names, such as Stilton cheeses, Newcastle Brown Ale and Jersey Royal potatoes. ·

good faith An obligation to act with honesty and openness. Various EU directives, such as the Commercial Agents Directive (86/653), require that individuals or businesses act with good faith in relation to others, and failing to do so can lead to a breach of the relevant directive and implementing national law. The concept is familiar to many continental EU jurisdictions.

GSP *See Generalised System of Preferences*.

green currency Payments to farmers under a Common Agricultural Policy system which provides for conversion from ECUs into national currencies.

Green Paper A consultation paper issued by an EU body, usually the Commission, setting out its preliminary views as to the form which future legislation will take. For example, in 1995 the Commission issued a Green Paper on the protection of utility models in the Single Market to solicit views on whether the Commission should propose harmonisation legislation in this area and if so what form it should take. The Commission is increasing its issue of Green Papers to ensure greater public consultation of proposals.

grey market goods *See parallel imports*.

group exemption *See block exemption*.

guarantee   A promise or warranty that in the event of a failure of goods to meet a required standard they will be repaired or replaced. The Commission has proposed a "Euro-guarantee", ie a guarantee to be provided with all consumer goods sold in the EU to be effective throughout the EU. However, such proposals have not got beyond the consultation stage.

Under EU competition law, where goods are sold throughout the EU under a network of distribution agreements, consumers buying products from one dealer in the network may have them repaired by any other distributor. However, distributors are also allowed to offer guarantees to their own customers over and above the manufacturer's guarantee.

There is no legislative obligation to provide an express guarantee with goods, though many Member States' laws contain provisions implying obligations of quality into sale of goods contracts. Attempts to exclude these in contracts with consumers may be void under the Unfair Terms Directive (93/13).

guidelines   Written notes from the Commission intended to provide assistance to business in areas where the law is unclear. Guidelines have no legal force.

H

harmonisation   The process of legislative change initiated by the Commission to bring Member States' laws into line with each other as differing national laws and product standards result in distortions in the market. Harmonisation continues despite the official completion of the Single Market on 1 January 1993 and there are many areas where harmonisation has yet to be achieved.

hearing   A formal meeting when businesses can put their case to the European Commission, such as in relation to the competition rules when an investigation under Article 85 and/or 86 is initiated.

hearing officer   An officer of the European Court whose role was established in 1982 after criticism of the administrative nature of the decision-making process of the Commission in competition law cases. The hearing officer organises and chairs hearings, decides the date, duration and place of hearings, supervises preparation of minutes of hearings, and seeks to ensure protection of the interests of defendants. The hearing officer will prepare a report of the hearing and make recommendations as to the future conduct of the matter.

health and safety   The EU has a complex health and safety policy, principally comprising directives which must be implemented in Member States to harmonise the law in this area. Directives cover a broad field, including health and safety at work and the environment, dangerous substances, product liability, etc. The key directives in this field are the framework directives which lay down an outline of controls before more specific controls are agreed. The Single European Act 1986 placed health and safety legislation high on the EU list of priorities by new provisions inserted into the Treaty of Rome, Articles 8a, 8b and 8c.

Health and Safety Agency   Situated in Bilbao, this body was created by the EU with the aim of improving the exchange of information and experience in the field of health and safety at work. It has an administrative board of 27 members who serve as the decision-making body.

horizontal agreement   An agreement between companies at the same level of trade, such as between two or more manufacturers or wholesalers, distributors or retailers, rather than two different levels of trade, for example between manufacturer and distributor (*see **vertical agreement***). Horizontal agreements which are restrictive of competition may infringe the competition provisions of Article 85 of the Treaty of Rome. Most cartels are horizontal, though vertical agreements are also caught by the rules.

humanitarian aid   Financial and other assistance sent by the EU to areas of the world where famine or other disasters have occurred.

I

IGC   *See Inter-Governmental Conference.*

IMF   *See International Monetary Fund.*

implementation   The process by which a Member State brings an EU directive into force at national level. In the UK this may be done by statute (such as the Trade Marks Act 1994 which implemented the EU Trade Marks Directive (89/104)) or statutory instrument/regulation such as the Duration of Copyright and Rights in Performances Regulations 1995 implementing the EU Copyright Term Directive (93/98).

import   To bring goods or services into one country from another. Restrictions on imports are prohibited under the Treaty of Rome with certain exceptions such as on health and safety grounds. In the Single Market imports should be made freely without restriction under national or other law and without tariff barriers.

import duty   Payment required to be made to the state for importation of products, as distinct from excise duty which is set by each country separately and results in products such as tobacco varying in price throughout the EU. Importation without payment of national excise duty is permitted where goods are for personal consumption only.

indirect taxation   Taxation levied on sales rather than personal income, eg value added tax (VAT). The EU has a variety of harmonisation measures in this field particularly in relation to VAT, though full harmonisation has not yet been achieved. *See also **direct taxation, taxation**.*

industrial property   See *intellectual property*.

information society   A term referring to developments in the field of technology, telecommunications and computing bringing particular benefit to society.

insider dealing   Using inside knowledge about corporate matters to profit from movements on the Stock Exchange. Directive 89/298 of 17 April 1989 requires Member States to make insider dealing unlawful and to co-operate by exchanging information for enforcement. In the UK this was implemented on 1 March 1994 by the Criminal Justice Act 1993. Under the directive inside information is defined as information which relates to particular securities, may be specific or precise, has not been made public and if it were made public it would be likely to have a significant effect on the price of any securities.

Institutions of the European Community   Collective name for the Council of Ministers, the European Parliament, the European Commission, the European Court of Justice and the Court of Auditors.

intellectual property   Sometimes called industrial property, this comprises copyright, trade marks, patents, designs and registered design rights, plant variety rights, utility models and applications for the same and other similar rights. The EU has sought to harmonise legislation in this area including:
- computer software
- copyright term
- databases
- data protection
- supplementary protection certificates for pharmaceutical patents
- trade marks
- draft designs directive and regulation
- community trade mark
- proposals for a utility models directive
- plant variety rights directive

- semiconductor topography rights (for chips, application specific integrated circuits)
- satellite and cable broadcasting.

There are strict rules under Article 85 of the Treaty of Rome in connection with licensing of intellectual property rights, including the Technology Transfer Regulation (240/96) and Research and Development Regulation (418/85). Most intellectual property rights exist at national level only. *See also European patent, Community trade mark (CTM).*

Inter-Governmental Conference (IGC)   A conference between Member States' governments. Among other matters on the agenda, the IGC, starting in 1996, aims to examine and possibly amend the Treaty on European Union (Maastricht Treaty).

interim measures   Temporary sanctions imposed by the Commission on businesses in breach of the EU competition rules pending a final decision, to ensure that permanent damage is not done to the party who has complained of such a breach of the rules. The interim measures may consist of requiring the offending company to resume supplies of goods to the complainant or in some other way remedy the conduct which has been the subject of complaint.

Integrated Customs Tariff (TARIC)   A customs tariff setting out classifications for goods. Goods are classed under a variety of tariff headings and the commodity code number is added. The UK tariff sets out what rate of excise duty should apply and states the rate of VAT due on import of goods. Part of the tariff is a commentary on general customs and excise arrangements and procedures. EU regulation 2658/87 contains general rules for interpreting the nomenclature of the customs tariff.

internal market   The Single Market of the EU in which goods circulate freely.

International Monetary Fund (IMF)   An agency of the United Nations (not an EU body) set up in 1944 to ensure co-operation in the area of monetary matters at international level, including all EU Member States.

interoperability   Term used in the Software Directive (91/250). Computer programs may, in very limited circumstances, be decompiled or reverse-engineered by lawful users for a permitted objective only, ie to create a program which can be operated with the program decompiled.

INTERREG   An EU programme on transfrontier regions which provides structural funds for border areas.

inter-state trade   Trade between Member States. Agreements relating to imports or exports are highly likely to affect inter-state trade, but so might an agreement between two businesses situated in one Member State, depending on the terms or effect of the agreement between them.

intervention   Action taken to interfere in markets, such as to support prices in relation to the Common Agricultural Policy. Produce may be stored until prices alter, which in the past has led to butter or meat "mountains". Goods held in intervention in this way have now largely been dissipated.

INTRASTAT   A system to collect EU trade statistics. It covers the supply of goods only. Goods received from another EU country are classed as "arrivals" and goods delivered to another EU country are classed as "despatches".

J

joint tendering   Two or more companies together trying to obtain business, usually by way of a response to a formal invitation to tender. This occurs where separate companies each have only some of the products or services required by those putting the matter out to tender, but together they have the complete package. Joint tendering, particularly between competitors, may be anti-competitive and infringe the EU competition rules and should be handled very carefully. Collusive tendering is illegal where competitors divide between them tenders which are available and either do not bid or collaborate in agreeing the prices they will each include in their response to the invitation to tender. Fines of up to 10% of group worldwide annual turnover can be imposed for such practices.

joint venture   Collaboration, often by means of setting up a separate joint venture company in which all partners have shares, to enable resources and skills to be shared. Defined in Commission Notice of 31 December 1994 (OJ 1994 C385/1) as "undertakings which are jointly controlled by two or more other undertakings". In practice joint ventures encompass a broad range of operations, from merger-like operations to co-operation for particular functions such as research and development, production or distribution.

The Commission treats some joint ventures as mergers which fall within the compulsory notification provisions of the EU Mergers Regulation where they exceed the financial limits set out. Others are regarded simply as co-operative joint ventures.

jurisdiction An area in which a particular court has competence. Most commercial contracts will specify which courts have jurisdiction, or competence, to hear disputes which arise from the contract. In national law cases there is a right for the courts to refer questions of EU law to the European Court of Justice (ECJ) under Article 177 of the Treaty of Rome. The ECJ will then decide the matter referred to it and return the case to the national courts to handle the matter. The Commission is keen to encourage cases to be brought before the national courts and issued a notice to this effect on 23 December 1992. *See also* **Brussels Convention**.

Justice and Home Affairs Policy The Treaty on European Union (Maastricht Treaty) deals with both Common Foreign and Security Policy and Justice and Home Affairs Policy. The provisions of the treaty in this area identify areas of common interest which extend the power of the Commission to propose majority voting to certain issues. This can apply to matters of asylum policy, crossing of borders, immigration policy, drug addiction, combating fraud and judicial co-operation in civil matters where "the objective of the Union can be attained better by joint action than by members acting individually".

K

Kangaroo Group   An informal group of members of the European Parliament. Its aim is to obtain support from areas of industry to assist the lobbying of the Commission. It is based in the UK.

Know-how Regulation   A block exemption regulation (556/89) under the competition rules which was superseded on 1 April 1996 by the Technology Transfer Regulation (240/96). The regulations set out those provisions which are permitted under Article 85 in a know-how licence. Know-how is defined as a body of technical information that is secret, substantial and identified in any appropriate form.

KONVER Programme   An EU programme which provides assistance for defence areas to convert to non-defence work.

L

languages   The official languages of the EU are Danish, Dutch, English, Finnish, French, German, Greek, Italian, Portuguese, Spanish and Swedish.

level playing field   A term used to refer to the circumstances when the laws are the same in all EU states so that businesses can compete fairly. The Single Market programme was aimed at ensuring that a level playing field was achieved by harmonisation of laws throughout the EU.

levy   A payment or charge. In the context of the Common Agricultural Policy, levies are charged on imports of agricultural products to ensure that they reach the level of the EU price.

liability   The responsibility of any manufacturer of goods or supplier of services for damage that its product or service may cause to the consumer. The Product Liability Directive (85/374) (OJ 1985 L210) regulates the conditions under which manufacturers and suppliers are liable. It imposes strict liability without proof of fault where there are defects in a manufacturer's product even though there may have been no fault or negligence on its part. A producer is liable under the directive for damage caused by a defect in the product. This is liability for physical damage to persons or property.

licensing   Granting of rights to others to use the property of another person, usually for a limited period and subject to certain conditions. This includes intellectual property such as copyright or patents. The EU has detailed rules relating to the licensing of technology (*see also **Technology Transfer Regulation***).

Lomé Convention An association agreement between 68 African, Caribbean and Pacific (ACP) countries and the EU which provides for co-operation in matters of commerce between signatories. The original convention was signed in Lomé, capital city of Togo, in 1975 and there have since been three further conventions, the most recent signed on 15 December 1989. Called Lomé IV, it covers special tariff preferences for the ACP countries which are in turn bound to give EU products most favoured treatment, with the exception of trade preferences granted between themselves or to other developing countries.

Lugano Convention An agreement signed in 1988 by all Member States and EFTA states, including Switzerland. Very similar to the Brussels Convention, it ensures free movement of judgments between the contracting states as long as the Brussels Convention is not applicable.

Luxembourg, Treaty of A treaty which came into force in 1971 to increase the powers of the European Parliament over budgetary matters.

M

Maastricht Treaty   *See Treaty on European Union.*

Madrid Agreement   An agreement signed in 1891 in Madrid to provide protection for trade marks. Four countries were then signatories, but many more have since joined. It was revised in 1957, 1967 and 1979. The governing body of the agreement is the World Intellectual Property Organisation which drew up a protocol — a form of alternative agreement — so that the system could be accepted by more countries. All EU states have signed the protocol, except for Finland and Sweden who are expected to do so imminently.

measure having equivalent effect   A law or regulation in a Member State which has the same effect as a restriction on imports or exports. Such measures are contrary to Articles 30–36 of the Treaty of Rome, with certain exceptions, for example on health and safety grounds.

Member of the European Parliament   An elected politician who is voted by the citizens of the Member States to be a Member of the European Parliament (*see also* ***European Parliament***).

Member State   A country which is part of the European Union: Austria, Belgium, Denmark, Finland, France, Germany, Greece, Ireland, Italy, Luxembourg, Netherlands, Portugal, Spain, Sweden, UK. The original members of the then European Economic Community (EEC) were Belgium, Germany, France, Italy, Luxembourg and Netherlands. The UK, Denmark and Ireland joined on 1 January 1973. Greece joined on 1 January 1981,

Spain and Portugal on 1 January 1986 and Austria, Finland and Sweden on 1 January 1995.

memorandum   A written communication from the Council of Ministers or the European Parliament setting out their views in relation to a particular matter.

merger   Two or more companies or businesses coming together under single ownership. Mergers with a Community dimension must be approved in advance by the Commission under regulation 4065/89. The regulation will apply to purchases of shares or assets, or direct or indirect changes in control of a business.

Mergers Secretariat   Part of the Commission which is charged with ensuring compliance with the EU Merger Regulation. It handles notifications of mergers with a Community dimension.

minor agreement   An insignificant commercial agreement which the Commission has held does not fall within the competition rules. The Commission's notice of 1986, as amended, provides that such agreements are those where market shares are under 5% and joint group worldwide annual turnover does not exceed 300 million ECU. *See also* **de minimis**.

misleading advertising   Advertising which in any way, including its presentation, deceives or is likely to deceive the persons at whom it is aimed, and is likely to influence them in such a way that their spending behaviour as a result is likely to injure a competitor. This is defined in the Misleading Advertising Directive (84/450) (OJ 1984 L250/17) which requires Member States to harmonise laws in this area.

mutual recognition   The acceptance by one Member State of compliance with standards or qualifications set up in another. *See also* **Cassis de Dijon**.

N

NATO   *See **North Atlantic Treaty Organisation**.*

negative clearance   The procedure whereby the Commission will determine that an agreement notified to it under the competition rules of the Treaty of Rome does not infringe the rules. For agreements which do infringe the rules an exemption may be granted. Most notifications contain an application for both negative clearance, and, if the Commission determines that the rules apply, an exemption under Article 85(3).

negotiated procedure   The method under EU public procurement directives by which only certain companies are invited to tender for a particular contract. Under this procedure the contracting entity may choose from a number of candidates. This procedure may not normally be used except in the utilities sector and then under strict conditions. In rare cases this procedure may be used without publication of a tender notice.

new approach directive   A directive harmonising technical specifications which states essential requirements in areas such as health and safety, but does not define all the details. The new approach followed a change in Commission policy after a 1985 resolution.

New Community Instrument for Borrowing and Lending (NCI)   A fund set up in 1978 to raise funds for the financing of structural investment projects through the European Investment Bank.

no-challenge clause   A clause typically in an intellectual property licensing agreement which restricts the licensee from challenging in any way the licensor's patent or other licensed rights. Such clauses are often void under

Article 85. Under the Technology Transfer Regulation (240/96), if such a clause is included then application can be made under the opposition procedure, whereby if the agreement is notified to the Commission and no opposition received from the Commission within four months, it is deemed exempted. Alternatively, it is always lawful to provide that a licence will terminate in the event of such a challenge, therefore in practice a provision to that effect is usually included.

non-tariff barrier   A hindrance to trade other than a financial levy. This might be a technical requirement of one Member State not present elsewhere.

Nordic Council   A body comprising Aaland Islands, Denmark, Faeroes, Finland, Greenland, Iceland, Norway and Sweden, set up in 1952 to represent these countries in matters of common interest.

North Atlantic Treaty Organisation (NATO)   An organisation set up in 1949 for defence purposes. Belgium, Canada, Denmark, France, Iceland, Italy, Luxembourg, the Netherlands, Norway, Portugal, the UK and the USA were the original members, with Greece and Turkey joining in 1952, West Germany in 1955 and Spain in 1982. In 1990 the united Germany joined.

notice   A non-binding commission document often issued to explain further details of an EU competition regulations in relation to the following fields:
- co-operation agreements
- subcontracting agreements
- agreements of minor importance
- agency agreements
- the distinction between co-operative and concentrative joint ventures.

Notices are not binding on the Commission. However, in practice, it would be very rare for the Commission to depart from policies set out in a notice.

nuclear energy   *See EURATOM.*

O

OECD   *See **Organisation for Economic Co-operation and Development**.*

Official Journal of the European Communities   Otherwise known as OJ, this is the official publication of the EU in which all notices, regulations and directives appear. The "L" series contains legislation and the "C" series contains proposals, information and notices. In the UK both series may be obtained from Her Majesty's Stationery Office.

oligopoly   Control of a market by a small number of suppliers which may or may not lead to the operation of a cartel.

one stop shopping   Approval from one body instead of several, such as in relation to regulatory approvals for medicines in the EU. Under merger law this is the ability to be subject to one set of merger rules only at EU level, rather than a whole series of national merger laws (*see also **merger regulation***).

open exclusive licence   A licence of intellectual property rights which does not infringe Article 85 of the Treaty of Rome despite being an exclusive licence. Most exclusive licences are not "open" and thus need to benefit from individual exemption under Article 85(3) or a block or general exemption regulation.

Open Network Provision (ONP)   The EU telecommunications regime and directives in that area which aim to provide open access to telecommunications networks.

open procedure   The procedure under the public procurement directives by which all interested contactors, suppliers or service providers may submit tenders. This is to be contrasted with the restricted and negotiated procedures. This is arguably the fairest of the three procedures and the one which is used most often. Some public authorities or utilities to which these rules apply may find it more expensive and time consuming than the other procedures.

opposition procedure   A procedure set out in various EU block exemption regulations by which an agreement can be notified to the European Commission for exemption or negative clearance and under which, if no objection is received from the Commission within a specified period, the agreement is deemed exempted from the competition rules. The procedure is rarely used and the Commission considered abolishing it when revising the patent and know-how block exemption regulations into the single replacement Technology Transfer Regulation (240/96).

opinion   A written document setting out the views of an EU body such as the Economic and Social Committee or the Advocate General. Various EU institutions issue opinions on proposals for new EU legislation which are published in the Official Journal of the European Communities.

opt-out   A clause or provision entitling a Member State to avoid certain provisions of a treaty. The UK has an opt-out from certain provisions of the Maastricht Treaty, notably on economic and monetary union and the Social Chapter.

Organisation for Economic Co-operation and Development (OECD)   An organisation comprising the members of the EU, EFTA, Australia, Canada, Japan, New Zealand, Turkey and the USA which co-ordinates trade policy and aims to expand international trade. Article 231 of the Treaty of Rome requires the EU to establish close co-operation with the OECD to be set out in a common accord. This was done in 1960. The Commission is given the right to take part in the work of the OECD.

origin system   Payment of value added tax (VAT) under which goods will be taxed before export at the rate of the exporting Member State. The Commission expects Member States to change to the origin system of VAT by 1 January 1997 at the earliest. In the meantime, a transitional system based on the destination of goods is in force. *See also* **destination system.**

P

Package Travel Directive   Directive 90/314 — the Package Travel, Package Holidays and Package Tours Directive — harmonises the law in this area. In the UK it was implemented by SI 1992/3288 on 1 January 1993. The aim of the directive is to protect consumers by requiring accurate brochures, proper contracts and guarantees in the event of insolvencies.

Packaging and Packaging Waste Directive   Directive 94/62 (OJ 1994 L365/10) harmonises the law on waste and packaging in order to reduce waste and protect the environment by reducing the overall volume of packaging. Re-use of packaging is encouraged and so is recycling. Member States may impose stricter requirements than the directive provides for. The directive allows Member States to give companies a transitional period of up to five years from 30 June 1996 to comply with directive. Under the directive the principle of the "polluter pays" is included, by which the undertaking responsible for the pollution must take financial responsibility for its actions.

parallel import   A product bought in one state and imported into another by the purchaser, often to take advantage of price differences between states. Also known as grey market goods, parallel importation usually takes place outside supplier authorised official distribution networks. Measures taken to prevent parallel imports in the Single Market will infringe Article 85 of the Treaty of Rome. Whilst it is permitted to restrict an exclusive distributor from soliciting sales outside its exclusive area, absolute territorial protection may not be given, whether by contract terms or by conduct or oral arrangements.

Paris, Treaty of   The treaty signed in Paris on 18 April 1951 which formed the European Coal and Steel Community before the Treaty of Rome was signed. The aim of the treaty, which deals solely with coal and steel, is to ensure a free market for these commodities and it includes measures such as the prohibition of import and export duties. Many provisions in this treaty are similar to those in the Treaty of Rome. The Treaty of Paris expires in 2002.

Patent Convention   *See **European Patent Convention.***

Patent Regulation   A block exemption regulation under Article 85 of the Treaty of Rome which terminated on 31 March 1996 and was replaced by the Technology Transfer Regulation (240/96).

payment, cross-border   Money paid from one Member State into another. There are proposals to harmonise the law in this field in order to avoid the significant distortion of the Single Market which arises from the cost of cross-border payments in the absence of monetary union; at present it is possible for bank currency conversion charges to exceed the value of the payment to be made. A single currency would remove the issue altogether.

pensions   EU law requires that there should be no discrimination in the area of pensions. Many Member States' laws have provided for different retirement ages for men and women, which have been held to be discriminatory and contrary to EU law. In the UK, for example, the Government has had to alter the law to phase in an equal retirement age of 65 for men and women. The pension which a Member State pays is a matter for national law.

performing rights   Rights of performers such as musicians in their live performances. The Copyright Term Directive (93/98) (OJ 1993 L290/9) harmonised EU law in this area and was implemented in the UK on 1 January 1996 by SI 1995/3297. Performers' rights must be protected under national law. The right exists for 50 years from the end of the calendar year in which the performance takes place, or if during that period a recording of the performance is released, for 50 years from the end of the calendar year in which it is released.

petition   Citizens of Member States have the right to present petitions to the European Parliament which has a special petitions' committee for this purpose. The committee brings the matter before the Parliament or other relevant institution.

plant breeders' rights   An intellectual property right in breeds of plant which enables the owner to prevent others copying the breed. EU Regulation 2100/94 (OJ 1994 L227/1) adopted an EU-wide system of plant breeders' rights, which previously had only existed at national level. There is also an International Convention for the Protection of New Varieties of Plants 1961 (as amended).

plant variety rights   *See **plant breeders' rights**.*

POSEDOM Programme   A programme providing compensation to French overseas territories, the Azores, Madeira and the Canaries to compensate them for certain disadvantages which they suffer as a result of their remote and insular nature.

positive discrimination   The action of favouring one sex or race. Positive discrimination is usually illegal, but some programmes are permitted which encourage one disadvantaged sex or race. Hence, statements in advertisements to the effect that applications from women, for example, or ethnic minorities are particularly welcome are legal, but any choice of candidate for a post solely on the grounds of race or sex will not be permitted in most circumstances.

predatory pricing   The practice undertaken largely by dominant businesses of pricing below cost in an effort to drive competitors out of the market. Whilst smaller companies are entitled to price as they wish, provided this is not in collusion with other companies, dominant entities must comply with Article 86 of the Treaty of Rome and predatory pricing may be an abuse of a dominant position contrary to this provision. Companies can be fined for engaging in such practices.

preference   Better treatment usually by way of reduced tariffs given to one country over another, particularly in the context of international trade.

presidency   Leadership of the European Union. Member States take it in turns to hold the presidency of the EU for a period of six months. Turns are taken by alphabetical order of the countries concerned and meetings of the Council of Ministers are chaired by the relevant minister whose country holds the presidency. This gives each Member State the opportunity to put forward measures which they favour.

President   The current Commission President is Jacques Santer whose duties include leading the Commission and ensuring it fulfils its legal obligations. The President is chosen by the Member States. The Treaty of Rome contains provisions dealing with the President (Article 161).

price discrimination   Where the level of a charge is not directly related to its costs, such as where prices are reduced to drive out a new competitor. Companies in a dominant position must not abuse that position and may act contrary to Article 86 of the Treaty of Rome where they do not treat customers or suppliers alike in similar circumstances, particularly in relation to price.

privileged   A term applied to documents which cannot be used in court proceedings against the defendant, usually because they contain confidential advice given by a lawyer to his client and it would harm the interests of the defence if the prosecution were able to see such documents. Under EU competition law, advice from an outside lawyer to a client is privileged and the Commission may not use such documents. However, advice from a lawyer employed in-house is not privileged, which is why it can be advantageous to take external competition law advice and ensure that all letters containing such advice are marked "EC Advice — Confidential and Privileged". Such documents should be kept in a separate filing cabinet to which Commission officials would not be granted access when conducting a dawn raid.

proceedings   A court hearing or action. This may refer also to action against a Member State brought by the Commission for breach of EU law.

product liability   The responsibility of manufacturers for damage caused by their defective products. Liability under EU law is contained in the Product Liability Directive (85/374) which was implemented in the UK by the Consumer Protection Act 1987. The directive provides for strict liability, ie liability without fault, where it can be proved that a defective product has caused death or personal injury or damage to property.

product market   A market defined by product, eg "whisky", "cars" or "dishwashers", as contrasted with a geographical market, eg the UK, Germany. Market definition is important for a number of areas of EU law, particularly competition law and merger law. It is not always easy to define a product market. Definition by reason of whether alternative products may be substituted or regarded as such by consumers is a good test. Economics apply a range of tests to determine a product market including "cross price elasticity of demand", ie if the price of fresh orange juice is raised will sales of apple juice increase and thus determine whether orange and apple juice are in the same market?   This is an inexact science and makes the application of the competition rules uncertain in many cases where market definition is important.

professional qualifications   See *free movement of services*.

proportionality   Ensuring that a legislative measure at EU level is introduced only when it is appropriate to have a measure at that level. *See also subsidiarity*.

protectionism   Protecting the interests of a Member State or the EU as a whole by imposing trade barriers and customs duties to prevent imports from abroad. Protectionism is the opposite of free trade. The EU is part of the World Trade Organisation and seeks to ensure free trade not only between its members of the EU but also with third countries.

public procurement   Obtaining goods or services for the use of the public sector. Procurement in this sector is often formalised and the contracts can be large. Contracts will be advertised for formal tender. In the past it was found that most public contracts were placed with local suppliers and in the 1970s, directives were issued requiring that large value public supply and works contracts be advertised throughout the EU and be open to all who meet the requirements set out therein. These directives have been amended and revised and extended now to cover services and utility contracts also. (*See also **open procedure**.*)

Three alternative procedures are set out in the directives, but the basic principle is that for public works, supplies or services contracts or contracts with utilities whether in the public sector or not, in each case where the value of the contract is over a certain minimum financial level, then the contract must be advertised in the Official Journal of the European Communities and suppliers from all EU States be entitled to put in tenders.

The company winning the contract must be chosen fairly in accordance with formulae set down in the relevant directive and where the procedure is not followed there is a right to claim damages under separate remedies directives.

Q

qualifications   The EU has agreed various directives to ensure cross-border recognition of vocational and professional qualifications. *See also free movement of services.*

qualified majority   A means of voting whereby four fifths of the votes cast must be cast in favour for a motion to be passed. The Single European Act 1986 extended rights of qualified majority voting to ensure that some of those provisions which had previously required a unanimous vote and which therefore were often permanently held up in the system could be progressed, particularly with regard to the Single Market measures. In 1986 about 100 measures were taken by qualified majority and by 1990 majority voting was so commonplace that the Commission did not even record the number of decisions taken by that method.

quantitative restriction   A limit on volume of goods imported or exported — this is prohibited under Articles 30–36 of the Treaty of Rome *(see also Article 30).* Measures having equivalent effect are also banned. Such a restriction may be a national law which is applied in a discriminatory way against non-nationals.

quota   A limited quantity of goods which are permitted by a state for imports or exports. For example, the EU sets national quotas for fishing catch.

quorum   A minimum number of people who must be represented at a meeting before it may proceed so as to deal with business effectively. This varies between institutions and bodies.

R

racism   Discrimination on the grounds of race or nationality. *(See also **free movement of persons**.)* The Treaty of Rome ensures free movement of workers but there are no guaranteed freedoms from discrimination on grounds of race and religion at a European level.

rapporteur   A European Parliament or other official servicing a particular organisation or committee whose job it is to help discussions progress in connection with a particular matter and to prepare a report on it.

recommendation   A suggestion or proposed measure which has no binding force under Article 189 of the Treaty of Rome but serves as an encouragement to good practice in specific areas. The Commission makes recommendations, but although account will be taken of these, there is no legal obligation that they must be followed by the Member States.

reciprocity   The principle that one will treat someone in a particular way if one is so treated by them. This is relevant under EU law in relation to agreements which the EU has with third countries, particularly in relation to public procurement and free trade.

regional funds   Money made available by the Commission to assist disadvantaged areas. Funds are available where a project is commercially viable or creates or assists employment. Regional enterprise grants are also available for small firms or new businesses with fewer than 25 staff. *See also **European Regional Development Fund** and **structural funds.***

regulation   EU legislation issued by the Council of Ministers which have direct effect in Member States. The Council may empower the Commission to make a regulation in a prescribed framework. Article 189 of the Treaty of Rome provides that a regulation shall have general application. It shall be binding in its entirety and directly applicable in all Member States.

Regulations are published first as drafts in the Official Journal of the European Communities, and may at an earlier stage be the subject of a Commission Green Paper with consultation at national level. The final version is also published in the Official Journal of the European Communities.

remedy   Recourse if a law, contract or duty is broken, usually the right to claim damages or obtain an injunction. Under the EU public procurement rules there are individual remedies directives setting out the rights of those injured through a breach of the rules to seek redress. Where a Member State fails to implement an EU directive or does so incorrectly where the directive was clear, those who have suffered loss as a result have the remedy of suing the relevant government for damages.

resale price maintenance   Action of a supplier in requiring its customer (usually a dealer or distributor) to sell the products purchased at prices stipulated by the supplier. This is contrary to Article 85 of the Treaty of Rome and most national competition law regimes. The Net Book Agreement of the UK, under which publishers may require that books be sold at listed prices, is being challenged under these provisions . Maximum resale prices are not as objectionable but still may be subject to challenge under EU law.

research and development   Developing technology through research. The EU has various programmes to encourage research and will supply funding for certain projects. EU Regulation 418/85 (OJ 1985 L53/5 as amended later) sets out how joint research and development agreements are treated under the competition rules. Research collaboration can restrict competition. Thus Article 85 may apply to such arrangements unless they comply with this regulation. The regulation expires on 31 December 1997. *See also **Fourth Framework Programme**.*

resolution   A decision of the European Parliament which approves a vote after a report or a Commission decision. The Council of Ministers may also make resolutions.

restricted procedure   A method under EU public procurement directives by which those responding to invitations to tender are chosen to win a particular contract. Under this procedure the contracting entity may choose from a number of candidates.

right of establishment   The right of nationals of Member States, under Article 52 *et seq* of the Treaty of Rome, to work and live in other Member States. *See also* ***free movement of persons.***

Rome, Treaty of   The treaty founding the European Economic Community (now the European Community and part of the European Union). The treaty was signed in Rome on 25 March 1957 by its founder members: Belgium, Germany, France, Italy, Luxembourg and the Netherlands. It is known also as the Treaty Establishing the European Economic Community. It has since been amended by the Single European Act 1986 and the Maastricht Treaty.

S

Santer, Jacques   The President of the European Commission.

SAVE Programme   The Special Action Programme for Vigorous Energy Efficiency, a programme which aims at ensuring energy saving.

Schengen Agreement   An accord to abolish controls at EU frontiers. It was initially entered into by the Benelux countries, France and Germany, followed by Italy, Spain and Portugal. The UK has reservations about the agreement because of concerns over illegal immigration, drug trafficking, terrorism and the spread of rabies. Iceland and Norway have associate membership, Denmark, Sweden and Finland have begun association negotiations.

second-hand goods   Value added tax (VAT) rules exist at EU level in connection with second-hand goods. A series of EU VAT rules have been agreed. In 1994 agreement was reached on common treatment of imports and sales of works of art and other antiques.

security policy   *See **Common Foreign and Security Policy (CFSP)**.*

selective distribution   The practice of appointing only certain distributors to a distribution network who comply with stated criteria. Thus cheap chain stores could be refused supplies of products through the authorised network of distributors. This may be anti-competitive and in breach of Article 85 of the Treaty of Rome. However, the Commission and European Court of Justice have permitted selective distribution where this can be objectively justified, such as where customers will need after sale services which they would not obtain from a cheap chain store where staff are untrained.

It has been permitted in a range of industries including motor vehicles, electronics, computers and cosmetics.

services   The provision of a facility other than goods. Services are regulated by the Treaty of Rome much in the same way as goods, however, there are some differences between goods and services in EU legislation. For example, the rules of the Commercial Agents Directive (86/653) apply only to agents who market goods, not services.

sex discrimination   The practice of favouring one sex above the other, often in employment matters. Sex discrimination is likely to break the law. Many cases involving sex discrimination have been brought from the national courts to the European Court of Justice. Article 119 of the Treaty of Rome provides that each Member State must ensure that men and women receive equal pay for equal work. Each Member State should have enshrined these provisions into national law.

These principles have been significantly clarified in recent years through a whole series of European Court of Justice cases in this field. These cases held that longer qualifying periods for part-time workers before they can claim unfair dismissal under UK law was discriminatory and that imposing a financial limit of about £11,000 under UK law where dismissal was discriminatory was a breach of EU law as were different retirement ages for men and women.

SE   See **Societas Europea**.

Single Administrative Document (SAD)   One document required to ship goods within the EU, ensuring that there is no need to have documentation which differs between Member States. The SAD will be acceptable in all states and is an export, transit and import declaration.

single currency   A currency valid throughout the EU. An aim of the Maastricht Treaty was to bring about a single European currency. The name "euro" has been agreed for the currency and in April 1996 the term "cent" was agreed for the coinage, but full monetary union appears several years away and may proceed with some members of the EU only (*see also* *Economic and Monetary Union* and *convergence criteria*).

Single European Act   The first act amending the Treaty of Rome in substantive fashion, signed in 1986. It came into force on 1 July 1987 and expanded the legal competence of the Community and its institutional structure. The Act adopted measures with the aim of establishing an internal market by 1 January 1993 (*see also* **Single Market**). The requirement for unanimity of voting in the Council of Ministers was replaced with qualified majority voting and improved the powers of the European Parliament. It introduced into the Treaty of Rome the first reference to the European Monetary System which had operated since 1979. It introduced provisions on political co-operation for the first time.

Single Market   The internal market in which goods and services may pass from one Member State to another without barriers to trade. The 1985 White Paper listed 265 measures to ensure a level playing field within the EU. *See also* **Cockfield, Lord.**

small and medium-sized enterprises (SMEs)   Independent companies with not more than 25% being owned by one or more large companies, having fewer than 250 employees and an annual turnover of less than 40 million ECU (£32 million). SMEs are encouraged by the Commission through various aid programmes.

Social Charter   The Community Charter of Fundamental Social Rights which was signed at the December 1989 summit by 11 out of the then 12 Member States. The effect of the UK's failure to agree was that the charter became non-binding. It includes an action programme with many proposals for directives and regulations on social policy.

Social Chapter   The Agreement on Social Policy reached by the same 11 Member States as signed the Social Charter. It is contained in an appendix to the Maastricht Treaty on European Union and supplements the original chapter on social policy in the Treaty of Rome. The objectives of this measure are to promote employment, improve living and working conditions, implement proper social protection and develop human resources with a view to lasting high employment. The social provisions include the minimum wage and the principle of equal pay for male and female workers for equal work. The UK has opted out of this.

Societas Europea (SE)   A European company, ie a legal entity which is formed under EU law rather than national law. A European company will only be defined as such where two companies merge or form a joint subsidiary and where there is a cross-border element. One company could do this if, for example, it has a subsidiary or branch in another Member State. The aim of the measure is to enable EU companies to pool resources and better compete against US and Japanese corporations. The Commission adopted an amended proposal on 22 May 1991 (COM (91) 174). The measure was first proposed in the 1970s and has still not yet been agreed.

Software Directive   Directive 91/250 (OJ 1991 L122/42) on the legal protection of computer programs (implemented in the UK by SI 1992/3233 from 1 January 1993) which provides that all Member States must protect computer programs by copyright law. The directive also provides a right to make back-up copies of software and a very limited decompilation right to reverse engineer software in order to write interoperable programs. A right to repair is also included unless a software licence prohibits this.

Spearhead   A computer database run by the UK Department of Trade and Industry. It summarises all current and prospective EU measures in the Single Market programme and in other areas which will have substantial implications for business.

specialisation regulation   An EU competition regulation which regulates agreements between companies under which they agree to collaborate and then specialise in particular areas. Such agreements may be anti-competitive in their effect and infringe the competition rules in Article 85 of the Treaty of Rome and Regulation 417/85 (OJ 1985 L53/1) provides a block or general exemption for such agreements. The regulation was amended in 1993.

standardisation   The process of agreeing standards. In the UK the British Standards Institution (BSI) has responsibility in this area. In the EU Euro Norms are agreed. Harmonisation of standards at EU level helps ensure a level playing field in the Single Market and is something which the Commission is keen to encourage. *See also* **Euro norm, CEN** *and* **CENELEC.**

state aid   Aid granted by a Member State or through state resources which distorts or threatens to distort competition by favouring certain undertakings or the production of certain goods. In other words, government assistance, often to national businesses, which is usually of a financial nature and discriminates against other businesses in competition with them. Articles 92–94 of the Treaty of Rome and provisions in the European Coal and Steel Community Treaty contain provisions regulating the granting of such aid. Article 92 prohibits state aid, but the EU may approve certain types of state aid where it is deemed beneficial.

statement of objections   A document issued by the Commission in a competition law investigation stating the case against the parties. They have an opportunity to reply and may ask for an oral hearing to put their case. The statement will set a time limit for a reply which can be extended and the Commission must provide a reasonable period in which to reply, usually two or three months.

structural funds   Financial aid from the EU aimed at reducing regional disparities. The funds comprise:
- the European Regional Development Fund
- the European Social Fund
- the European Agricultural Guidance and Guarantee Fund
- the Financial Instrument for Fisheries.

subcontracting   Arranging for work to be undertaken by a third party. The Commission defines such agreements in its notice of 18 December 1978. The Commission does not believe that such arrangements generally can breach the EU competition rules in Article 85 of the Treaty of Rome and sets out in detail in its notice which provisions are permitted in such agreements.

subsidiarity   The principle that legislation should be undertaken at the most effective level, whether it be local or regional government, national or EU level.

supremacy   The principle that EU law prevails over national law. There are many instances of national law being overturned by the European Court of Justice when a Member State has ignored provisions of the Treaty of Rome.

SWIFT   A computer system which links many banks in the EU and permits information and payment to be transmitted electronically.

T

takeover *See **merger**.*

taxation Income from individuals and businesses to fund the state. Article 100a of the Treaty of Rome gives Member States the right to veto EU initiatives in the field of taxation and this has prevented harmonisation of direct taxes. However, indirect tax in the form of value added tax has been the subject of some harmonisation.

technical barrier A barrier to trade caused by differing national technical specifications for products, such as testing. Such a barrier may be a quantitative restriction on imports or exports and is prohibited by Articles 30–36 of the Treaty of Rome.

Technology Transfer Regulation EU Regulation 240/96 (OJ 1996 L31/2) which provides block exemption protection from Article 85 (competition law) for certain categories of patent and know-how licence (and trade mark, design, copyright and other intellectual property licences which are ancillary to a patent or know-how licence). From 1 April 1996 the regulation replaced earlier regulations on patent and know-how licensing. It applies to new licences entered into after that date and sets out those provisions which are permitted, those which are exempted and those which are prohibited (or black-listed).

The Commission retains a residual right to withdraw the benefit of the regulation where the licensee's market share exceeds 40% and in certain other defined circumstances. This and other block exemption regulations made under the competition rules is very useful for those drafting such agreements.

telecommunications   The EU has various initiatives in the field of telecommunications. It has agreed widespread harmonisation of technical standards and liberalisation of telecommunications which will require Member States to allow competition in the telecommunications area.

Tenders Electronic Daily (TED)   A computer database which contains information of all EU contracts available for tender under the EU public procurement directives. These are also published in the Official Journal. TED is updated daily and is accessible through a number of sources, including all UK Euro Info Centres. The database can be searched by various criteria, including sector, country and date.

territoriality   Territory, area and regionalism; also used to denote the requirement that heavy goods vehicles and lorries are required to pay taxes based on the roads they use, not their nationality.

third country   A country not a member of the EU.

TIR Convention   Transport International de marchandises par Route (international transport of goods by road), part of the Geneva Convention 1975 on the international transportation of goods by road.

Toy Safety Directive   Directive 88/378 sets out legal requirements in relation to the safety of toys. This includes the requirement to apply the CE marking to toys to indicate compliance with the directive. *See also **CE marking** and **product liability***.

trade associations   Associations of interested persons representing those involved in a particular trade. Such bodies may make representations to the Commission on proposed EU legislation affecting their area of trade. Trade associations need to be particularly careful not to infringe the EU competition rules; many large companies have written policies telling their members what they can and cannot discuss at trade association meetings. Associations can collect statistics about members, but any dissemination must not reveal the members by name if the matter concerns prices, terms of business and similar issues.

trade mark A registered or unregistered sign indicating a connection between traders and their goods. The law relating to trade marks has been harmonised in the EU by the Trade Marks Directive (89/104) (OJ 1989 L40/1) which was implemented in the UK by the Trade Marks Act 1994. EU-wide trade marks known as Community trade marks (CTMs) have been available since 1 April 1996 under Regulation 40/94 (OJ 1994 L11/1). *See* ***Community trade mark*** *and* ***Madrid Agreement.***

Trade-related Aspects of Intellectual Property Rights (TRIPS) The intellectual property rights agreement which arose from the Uruguay round of international trade talks (*see* ***General Agreements on Tariffs and Trade (GATT)*** *and* ***World Trade Organisation (WTO)***). TRIPS sets out how participating nations will protect intellectual property rights: some provisions of the Berne Convention (1971) on copyright will be complied with, computer programs should be protected as literary works and databases by copyright and other matters. Trade marks and patents should be protected in accordance with the Paris Convention for the Protection of Intellectual Property with additional protection for designs and the layout of integrated circuits and for plant variety rights.

Developed countries were given until 1 January 1996 to bring legislation into conformity with TRIPS. Developing countries were given until 2000 and the least developed countries an additional six years.

transfer of undertakings The sale of a business to a third party. The Acquired Rights Directive (77/187) requires that Member States protect the employment rights of individual employees when such a transfer occurs. The new employer must take into account employees' accumulated redundancy rights and unfair dismissal rights. In the UK this directive has been implemented by the Transfer of Undertakings (Protection of Employment) Regulations 1981 which have since had to be amended to reflect EU law accurately. There have been many legal cases on what exactly is a "transfer of an undertaking" particularly in relation to contracting out of local government services.

transparency   Ensuring that those operating in a particular market are able to see clearly the rules to which they are subject and the reasons behind such measures. A wider meaning refers to the whole European law-making process and enabling the ordinary citizen to understand this process.

Treaty on European Union (Maastricht Treaty)   Signed at Maastricht, this treaty expanded the scope of the responsibilities of the European Community and brought in new policy areas, including the Common Foreign and Security Policy and Justice and Home Affairs Policy. The treaty is a further step in the process of creating an ever closer union of the peoples of Europe and has goals such as improving economic progress, establishing a single currency and eventually a common foreign and defence policy. The UK opted out of various parts of the treaty including the Social Chapter and various economic and monetary union issues. The treaty has been in force since 1 January 1993.

TRIPS   *See Trade-related Aspects of Intellectual Property Rights.*

troika   A system by which the countries who hold the immediate past and immediate future presidencies of the EU act as a team with the current country in office to ensure continuity.

turnover   Sales of goods or services of a company. Turnover is defined in detail in the EU Merger Regulation and there is a separate notice under that regulation on the calculation of turnover (OJ 1994 C385/21) . Other competition law regulations have provisions relating to turnover, for example the Minor Agreements Notice which suggests that the competition rules do not apply to undertakings where their aggregate worldwide group annual turnover does not exceed 300 million ECU and market share is under 5%. Reference should be made to the relevant EU regulation for the precise definition of turnover in each case.

tying clause   A clause in a commercial agreement requiring the purchaser or licensee to purchase products other than those which are the subject matter of the agreement. This may be a requirement to buy unrelated products to ensure the supplier is able to supply a full range of goods ("full line forcing").

Dominant companies imposing ties may infringe Article 86 of the Treaty of Rome as an abuse of a dominant position and need to exercise particular caution.

U

Universal Copyright Convention (UCC)   A convention on copyright which seeks to set out common rules for recognition of copyright of another country. The UCC was set up to bridge the gap between those countries which had signed the earlier Berne Convention and those signing a Pan-American Convention on copyright. It was signed at Geneva in 1952 and revised in Paris in 1971. The UCC, unlike other conventions in this area, requires that the copyright sign © appears, and it also provides for registration of copyright. It provides for a minimum term of copyright of the life of the author plus 25 years. It is not an EU measure. The US joined the Berne Convention under its Paris revisions in 1979 from 1 March 1989.

United Nations (UN)   An international organisation based on equality of nation states. Its charter calls for the maintenance of international peace and security, and achievement of international co-operation and solving of problems and respect for human rights. The original charter, which came into effect on 24 October 1945, was signed by 51 nations. In May 1994 there were 184 members.

undertaking   A business, including a limited company, partnership or sole trader. EU case law has established that some state bodies which are of a trading nature, charities and trade associations may under certain circumstances be classed as undertakings.

unemployment   Lack of paid work for those who want it. The EU seeks to minimise unemployment. It has a system of grants and regional funds to aid depressed areas and stimulate the economy thus providing more jobs.

unfair competition   Using economic power to prevent traders competing in the normal course of business; also used for a specific legal wrong in many continental jurisdictions separate from, but related to, competition law. The UK has no equivalent, simply having the tort of passing off which prevents close copies of a product whether the trade mark protecting it is registered or not. In the general sense the EU has competition rules, as do many Member States in their national law.

unfair contract terms   Terms which are one sided or unfair. In consumer contracts these may be held unenforceable because of the provisions of Unfair Contract Terms Directive (93/13) (OJ 1993 L95/29) as implemented into national law in the Member States. The UK implemented this measure on 1 July 1995 by SI 1994/3159 which applies in addition to the Unfair Contract Terms Act 1977. The directive contains a list of terms which may be unfair. It only applies to consumer contracts. National laws may prohibit unfair terms in non-consumer contracts if they so wish.

UNICE   *See **Union of Industrial Federations of the European Community**.*

Union of Industrial Federations of the European Community (UNICE)   An EU-wide body representing employers of which the UK Confederation of British Industries and other similar national EU employers' bodies are members. UNICE lobbies in relation to new EU legislation and other matters in order to further the interests of its members.

utilities   Telecommunications, gas, electricity, water and similar services, often provided by state bodies though originally in the private sector and now, in Member States such as the UK, largely returned to private ownership. Article 90 applies to such bodies and the Commission has individual policies in areas covered by utilities. In addition, large value contracts in the utilities sector must be advertised and open to all through-out the EU. The EU is seeking the liberalisation of the utilities and is in the process of setting deadlines for competition in these areas where in most Member States competition has traditionally been prohibited.

V

VAT regime   A common system of rules on value added tax has been agreed by various EU Directives which must be implemented into national law in the Member States. There is a highly complex set of provisions in this area. Article 99 of the Treaty of Rome required the EU to adopt harmonisation measures for turnover taxes, excise duties and other forms of indirect taxation, but only "to the extent that such harmonisation is necessary to ensure the establishment and functioning of the internal market". The legislation is based on the first VAT Directive (67/227) (OJ 1967 71/1301) and the sixth VAT Directive (77/388) (OJ 1977 L145/1) with considerable amendments and supplementary provisions added later.

VDU Directive   *See Visual Display Screen Directive.*

vertical agreement   An agreement between businesses at different levels of trade such as between supplier and distributor or wholesaler and retailer. (*See also horizontal agreement.*) The EU competition rules apply to both vertical and horizontal agreements though many vertical agreements benefit from block exemption protection.

vertical restraint   *See vertical agreement.*

veto   A right to block a piece of legislation where unanimous voting is required. *See also qualified majority.*

Visual Display Screen Directive   Directive 90/270 sets out requirements for matters such as risk assessments of computers used at work, provides for free sight test and footstools for staff and regular breaks from VDU work.

void Of no effect and therefore unenforceable. Article 85(2) provides that agreements which restrict competition are void. Each Member State's law determines whether in the context of competition law this means the whole agreement is unenforceable or just the relevant clause. In most states it is simply the offending clause which cannot be enforced through the courts.

voting A process to choose a government or other body or pass a legislative measure. *See **veto** and **qualified majority**.*

Every citizen of the EU is entitled to vote in elections for the European Parliament.

W

waste control   Environmental measures to control the creation, treatment and movement of waste. The EU agreed a framework directive on waste (75/442) (OJ 1975 L194). Many other directives have since been agreed such as on waste oils, PCBs/PCTs, toxic and dangerous waste, sewage, batteries, hazardous waste, etc. *See also* ***Packaging and Packaging Waste Directive.***

Western European Union (WEU)   An association of European countries founded in 1955 by the UK, France, Belgium, the Netherlands and Luxembourg, Italy and Germany. Portugal and Spain were admitted in 1988 and Greece in 1992. Its military functions are performed by NATO and its economic activities mostly by the European Community. Its social and cultural activities were transferred to the Council of Europe in 1960. Its principal function now is to provide a forum for views on defence and foreign policy. Meetings are held twice a year at ministerial level and twice a month at ambassadorial level. It has several permanent agencies to assist with its work and its headquarters are in Brussels.

white clause   A clause in a commercial agreement which does not infringe the competition rules, usually set out in an EU block exemption regulation. Opposite of black clause.

White Paper   A document setting out proposals at national or EU level which may result in legislative or other change. A white paper usually follows a Green Paper, or preliminary document. The White Paper will contain more detail and alterations to the original proposal and takes account of views received in relation to the Green Paper. The White Paper may or may not result in a change in the law.

WIPO *See World Intellectual Property Organisation.*

World Intellectual Property Organisation (WIPO) An agency of the United Nations based in Geneva which co-ordinates intellectual property rights matters on a worldwide basis. Not an EU institution.

worker participation. Giving employees a say in the running of their employer's business. The Social Chapter of the Maastricht Treaty requires the setting up of works councils as part of an employee information and consultation procedure. The UK has opted out of this, but some UK companies which operate throughout the EU are setting up or have set up such consultation arrangements in the UK as well as other parts of the EU.

working group Small committees drawn from larger consultative bodies to discuss specific topics or to meet with Commission officials.

works council *See European Works Council. See also worker participation.*

World Trade Organisation (WTO) This body emerged from the Uruguay round of trade talks under General Agreements on Tariffs and Trade (GATT) which was then restructured and called the WTO. It began operation on 1 January 1995 and is headed by a ministerial conference. It has a secretariat which handles its day-to-day work. Each member participating in the WTO Agreement (at least 111 states) agrees to conform to the various GATT agreements.